MOTOCROSS: HEART OF A RACER

MOTOCROSS: HEART OF A RACER

AN INSIDERS VIEW OF THE WORLD OF MOTOCROSS AND A DEEP LOOK INTO THE MIND OF ONE OF IT'S CHAMPIONS

KENT WALKER

Printed in the United States of America

First Printing, 2017

ISBN-13: 978-1-945949-92-0

Waterfront Digital Press
2055 Oxford Ave
Cardiff, CA 92007

http://www.waterside.com/

CHAPTER 1
DOWN AND DIRTY

In the brief moment between waking up and opening my eyes for the first time of the new day my mind races with a single relentless thought. "It's race day!" I lie there for a while waiting for the grogginess of slumber to wear off. Looking up I don't see the popcorn ceiling. I see the motocross dirt track I'll be tearing to shreds with my modified Suzuki 250 in several hours.

Swinging my legs off the bed, standing up and struggling to pull my jeans on silently to avoid waking up my wife, I remember fuzzy images of the dreams from the night before. Jumping the motorcycle a hundred feet through the air, calculating each attack of every corner to get the best lap time and how to intimidate my competitors, which are just as focused as me and often times just inches away as we speed through the track at over fifty miles an hour, with every tool I can use. Over and over I have already finished the race in my mind, but soon it's going to be real. The dreams won't matter anymore.

I remind myself, "I'm here to win." Then I smile and think, "And I will." That's my only option.

Motocross racing is the single-most physically demanding sport on the planet. It also requires an extreme mental toughness that few can achieve. Imagine standing in the middle of a heavy weight boxing ring taking on Mike Tyson and playing a game of chess against the world's best player at the same time. If you can grasp what that would feel like, you are about half way to understanding the stresses motocross puts on the body and mind. And it's fun to watch. The sport has grown in popularity tenfold over the last couple of decades.

Contributing factors like cable TV multiplying the number of channels your TV can receive and the need to fill extra air time, Speed TV, the X Games, and many other factors have catapulted the sport into the public eye. Not a day goes by that you can't find the sport in one variation or another on television. On the slow sport days you have a better than even chance that clips of the flying bikes will be on the big screen TVs at sport bars across the country. It also fills stadiums, in many countries, with the most awesome fans in the world. While top riders do not become household names like Tiger Woods or Michael Jordon, they do enjoy nothing short of a rock star status in the unique sub-culture. I can tell you first hand that people idolize you when you're a top rider. The admiration, the money and recognition can be mind boggling. It's also addicting.

But before any rider has a chance to reap the reward of a successful career in motocross, a high price must be paid. I know because I have paid it. I am twenty eight years old and can honestly tell you that there is absolutely nothing else I have ever wanted to do as much as mastering the bike and track in front of the crowds. No rush can compare to it. The pride and sense of accomplishment are immeasurable and, knowing from firsthand experience, I can tell you that all the sacrifices that have to be made to become a top rider are worth it — most of the time.

All the time spent at the gym, practicing on the track and living a life that revolves around the micro-world of motocross boils down to one day. Race day. The day the hard work pays off or dreams are crushed. There can only one "best" and I have never liked the idea of being "second best" so I learned early on in my career that if you want to beat out the competition for the top spot you have to want it more and be willing to do anything to get it. No one ever won a race by relying on excuses or not trying hard enough.

You might think that the race starts when the gate drops, unleashing the motorcycles and riders on the twenty-minute quest to see who is the fastest. For many of the other riders that may be true. They will relax and shoot the crap with some of their buddies until race time. Others may rest, play video games or listen to their iPods. Then there's me. My race starts the millisecond my feet hit the floor getting out of bed. My mental gears rev up as I look for any and every angle I can use to my advantage. I honestly believe that I bring to the sport a mental intensity that is unmatched by any of my competitors. Some may think that I am arrogant. They are wrong. I'm confident and confidence is what wins races.

Like I mentioned before, the mental intensity is vital to win. On the flip side I know that if I can mess with the other racers' minds I have even more of an advantage. All the people who know me consider me to be a nice guy. I love to laugh, have fun and joke around. My youngest sister, Nina, still makes me blush when I hear her describe me to others. "Oh, he is such a sweetheart!! The most awesome brother in the world…" I still get embarrassed just thinking about it.

On the morning of the race I'm still a nice, fun loving guy, but now I have a purpose and those who are closest to me know that there is a reason for everything I say and do. The people who do not know me well have no idea. That gives me an advantage from the start. The mind games I play can be very subtle or incredibly intense. It all depends on the moment, the person, and what I want to accomplish.

Just after I suit up in my racing gear and just before I head out to the pits I fill up my water bottle. I always have it with me.

The clear plastic container displays a strangely colored liquid and people are always asking, "What's in the bottle?"

Sometimes I'll say, "Dude, I came up with this new mixture of all this different stuff! I can't believe how great it is. Maybe I should market it and put Rock Star to shame!"

Sometimes I tell them it's Kool-aid. I have a bunch of bogus answers in my pocket ready to toss out at an instant. All in all I'm just having fun with it. But, as I leave the other riders behind me walking towards the track I can hear them talk amongst themselves asking each other what they think is in my bottle. My mission accomplished, I smile. If they are thinking about what's in my bottle, they are not thinking about the race. I am.

Some would say, "Come on, that can't help you..." But they don't understand that motocross is a sport of inches and half seconds. Many times that's the difference between winning and not winning and I know from experience that the rider who is the most focused on the checkered flag is the one most likely to have it waved signaling his victory. So, I use whatever tool I can think of to gain the advantage. If I can distract the other riders' focus for just a few moments and maintain my focus on winning, I win. By the way, I fill my bottle with Gatorade diluted with lots of water. That's the big secret of the mystery liquid. To all of my competitors who might be reading this: Don't worry, I have plenty more secrets in my arsenal.

Mental intensity, physical condition, mechanical precision, emotional focus, creative techniques, and strategies. These are just some of the tools of my trade and I have learned and am always learning how to master them all. Of course I still stick to the basics. I make sure I eat the right foods to ensure a high level of energy and mental clarity. I make sure to get the rest I need and stay fully hydrated. I have seen what happens to other racers who don't pay attention to these details. Those are the one who finish races at the back of the pack, if at all.

This sport is also a money sport. There is a lot of money to be made and it takes a lot of money to compete. Because of this fact it is customary and expected that I work the crowds at the track before the race. I do this partly to show the fans my appreciation, but mainly to search out, find and reel in the Holy Grail for all motocross racers. Sponsors. I fully understand the importance of the business aspects of this great sport and there are no words that can express how much I appreciate the fans. I love them all, but on race day it can be a challenge to fulfill the responsibilities of keeping the fans and sponsors happy and maintaining the focus I demand of myself to win the race that is now less than two hours away. I wish I had a dollar for every time I would tell someone, "Hi! I'm Derek Costella, nice to meet you!" If I did, I wouldn't need sponsors in the first place. But, I'm sure glad the sponsors and fans are there. Without either of them there would not be a race.

As the clock ticks toward start time I get a chance to walk the tract. No two are the same. Differences in the consistency of the dirt, slopes of the high-banked turns and the distances of the jumps are just a few of the variables. In most racing sports there is the luxury of having tried the track before. Race after race it remains basically the same. Not in this one. Every race, even every lap, leaves its mark on the track. The spinning knobby tires cut deep new ruts with each pass and the flying dirt constantly changes the feel. You really are racing on the track for the first time, every time. That's just one of the things that make the sport so mentally challenging—you always have to make adjustments. But I can still set my basic strategies. I get to know every turn and jump and embed them into my brain. I also look for the rhythms and hidden secrets that other riders often miss. After a little time of inspection I can close my eyes tight and draw you an accurate picture of how the track lays and exactly where the finish line is.

After the walk around the racers get to hit the track for the first time on their bikes. My mechanic rolls my Suzuki to the tract as I get ready for the practice run. Chad is one of my best friends and knows the sport as well as anyone. He has experience racing, but his true gift is building a bike that can survive the beating and win. It's not like you can go to the shop and pick out a bike off the showroom floor and expect to be able to be victorious. He gets the bike, tears it down to the frame and rebuilds it into a Thoroughbred. More horsepower, durability, and lighter weight are the priorities and I cannot begin to explain how important the result is. Chad is an artist at creating the balance.

If a bad rider is on a great bike he still will not win. The human element is too important. If a great rider races a crappy bike, he might be competitive, but not win, just finish in the top 20 per cent. To be champion material you have to be the best rider on the best equipment, plain and simple, and Chad takes the challenge as seriously as I do. While I'm playing the mind games with the other riders and getting psyched for the race he is going through the bike with painstaking detail. It's important. Even incorrect tire pressure can spell disaster. And these bikes are the real monsters. That Harley that scares the hell out of you with its loud rumbling exhaust as it passes you by on the highway couldn't survive one lap. The first jump alone would total it. But motocross racing is as hard on the bikes as it is on the riders, so I go through a lot of motorcycles. If they were women you could call me the biggest womanizer on the planet and I would be serving time for their abuse.

All the motorcycles are checked out by the officials to make sure they are race legal. They look them over to make sure they meet the safety requirements, which aren't much, and test the decibel level from the tail pipes. With this method they can tell the horsepower and if any of the racers are trying to sneak in a "Cheater Engine." All racers try to find advantages and sometimes their mechanics get over zealous on the power of the bikes. Sometimes this is where a rider's day ends. If the bike's power is just a fraction over what is allowed the judges tell the team to have a nice day and enjoy watching the races. "Sorry, but you won't be in them today."

I take the bike over from Chad and get ready for the first practice. The bike feels good, I feel good, and I am excited to get some fast laps completed so I can find the fastest "line" around the track. The front tires on the bike are about four inches wide and the back closer to seven inches. There is a line on every track that is most efficient and the path to victory. It's as wide as the back tire. Every rider looks for it, but most wait until the main race begins. I start now. You have to remember that I have already been completely focused from the moment I opened my eyes this morning. I have worked things out in my mind so I do not have to shake out any fears or look for some way to be more comfortable with the bike. I already know that I can do anything with my bike that anyone else can do. Even better than others. So on my practice run I'm not worried about how the bike feels. I have my eyes on the prize, the checkered flag that will be waving over the finish line of the big race in a couple of hours. The line, or "grooves" as others call it, can change many times during a race as I explained before. But I can get a general feel of where it should be. When the real race starts the other riders will be looking for the line as much me. But because of what I do in the practice laps my search will cover a path of inches compared to the other racers' foot-wide search.

I also allow myself to have some fun on these practice runs. After a few laps I have already put in some of the fastest times and do not want to show my secrets to the other riders. I know the stadium is already starting to fill with crowds of fans so I give them a little show here and there. I might throw some whips or tricks over a jump or hold on to a wheelie a little longer than I should. I'm getting into it and allowing myself to enjoy it too. But I can assure you I am still completely focused on finding and owning the line, figuring out where the sweet spots are on all of the lips and landings of the jumps and dissecting each corner to find the most speed.

After the practice sessions the qualifying heats begin. Things become more serious now. They are in no way as intense as the final race, but you do have to qualify. If you do, you race. If you don't, you go home. So I give it my all and qualify. It also gives me a heads up about the other racers. I can spot their strengths and weaknesses. I have been competing with a lot of these guys for a while, but no two weeks are the same. One guy's shortfall last week might be his strength this time around. Some are better at shooting out of the big corner and gaining that extra millisecond. Others are great at hitting the jumps perfectly and a few have a knack for entering the turns a little faster than others. Then you have those who seem to jump from the gate at the perfect moment. I have my own technique for that.

Being able to see how the other racers react to all the different situations in the qualifying heats gives me the edge I can use when the big race begins. The track has now started to change in a more consistent way, so it will be easier to keep my tires on the ever-changing line that I want, need to own.

After the qualifying heats I hand the bike back over to Chad who will again perform his magic and repair any damage from the laps from the practice and qualifying runs and search for anyway to tweak an extra ounce of torque or fraction of a horsepower from the two hundred pound Suzuki. He is just as focused as I am. It's not a good thing to have a mechanical failure on the tract, obviously. But in this sport the stakes are high. The condition of the bike will often be the difference between winning or losing. It also determines if you finish at all. It's no fun having to push your bike off the tract before the checkered flag comes out. It is even less fun to have the paramedics help you off the field because of an equipment failure. I know that the bike and I are in good hands with Chad, so now it's time for me to get myself into the mental zone I have been gearing up to all day.

Motocross is a team sport, but to be honest, in the hour before the race begins I don't think about that. Everyone has already done their jobs. The trainer's, promoter's, manager's and mechanic's control of the race is over and it is up to me now. I have the greatest team and feel lucky to have friends that I love to work with, but in these moments I have to focus on me so I don't let the team down.

Here my wife understands this more than anyone. Jackie will run a kind of interference for me. People will try to talk to me, and I'm still smiling and joking around, but I do not absorb what they are saying. Jackie will step in and save me by answering some of the questions. I have a friend who writes for one of the trade magazines. I remember one time walking into his den while he was hitting the keys on his computer to make a deadline. His daughter, Brandy, was pushing a vacuum cleaner around his feet finishing up her chores. I tried to say hello but got no response. I figured he couldn't hear over the loud roar of the appliance, so I waited in the patio. When he came out to join me a few minutes later I had to ask, "How can you concentrate on writing with that vacuum blaring right next to you?"

He looked confused as he asked, "What vacuum?"

That's how it is for me. I shrink into my own world where I am its only inhabitant. I won't let anything distract me from the goal at hand. With the bike ready and the race that's about to start, nothing else exists. I know it can be a little confusing for the people around me, but they understand that I have to focus on wining.

As I walk up to the starting line I see Chad going over the bike one last time. Its tank filled with racing fuel. At two hundred dollars for five gallons, I never complain about putting gas in my car. The bike is as good as it's going to get. The time is here.

I look at the other riders searching for any hint of where they are mentally. Some are nervously joking around. Others are engaged in quiet conversation. The ones I worry about are the ones who seem as focused as me, so I have to do something about it. I walk up and take the bike from Chad and act like I do not have a care in the world, all along thinking how can I mess with the minds of the other riders. I look at one of the quiet ones and say, "There's a lot of cute guys here!" My wife hates that one. I might look at a couple of the others and say, "Hey, can I borrow some gas, my mechanic forgot mine." It's different for the start of each race, but I always find ways to screw with the other riders' mindsets. Sometimes I just play it cool. A lot of these guys have raced with me before and it unnerves them to see me with something other than a happy go lucky attitude.

As the starting girl, also known as the thirty-second girl, is walking with the starting board to set up fifty yards in front of us, I'm moving my leg around. People who are watching assume that I'm taking a last stretch, but I'm not. With the heel of my racing boot I am carving deep C-shaped trenches in the dirt. Five or six deep under my bike without being noticed by the other racers. When the "thirty second to start" card goes up I back my bike so the back tire rests firmly in a trench. By this time the other riders are in their own mental world and do not notice. The ones that do notice realize what I am doing, but it's too late. My first edge.

I once trained with an ex-navy seal. This guy kicked my butt into shape one summer and explained to me that when I go into a race that I have to treat it like a war, a battle to the bitter end. He's right, it is that intense, and I have had to use my motorcycle as a weapon many times. No war has ever been won without proper planning and I believe and hope I have planned more than any other racer who will be on the track today. When the other riders were off doing their own thing between the qualifying runs

I was watching the start of the other races. The races start when the gate drops. Before that the starting girl turns the "30 Seconds Card" and I immediately look to the gate. There is a one to five second lapse between the moment the card drops and when the gates go down. The same guy stomps down on the bar that releases the gates every race of the day and becomes predictable with the timing. I learn when the gate is going to drop to the millisecond. The other riders wait to see the gate drop. My plan is to be rolling before it does. The hard part is maintaining the mental control. Ticking off a couple of seconds in my head might seem easy, but the adrenalin is now rushing through my body in a relentless siege. It has the ability to cloud my judgment and distort the small increments of time. So, I inhale a chest full of air and imagine blowing out some of the excess human speed from my system. I think it works.

In the few last few seconds before the start I make my mental checks. I can feel my rear tire planted in the trench I carved out. Now instead of flat dirt my back tire with its big knobbies will have much more of a bite at the start and I will get a better launch. This and my plan to get the jump by knowing before the other riders when the gate drops should give me at least a wheel-length advantage right away. A wheel length might not seem like a big deal, but believe me, it's a big deal. I have lost races by half a wheel length.

Moments to go. Time is warped by the energy and tension. I am aware that many of my competitors are friends, but friendship stops when the gates drop. One last time I go through the race in my mind. I try to plan the next twenty minutes inside of a few seconds. I feel good, I am clear and physically I am in the best shape of my life. It's the mental energy that I have to keep in check. My body will not falter until minutes after the finish line. My mental focus may not. In ten minutes I will have to focus on being focused.

The board drops. I count the time for the gate in my head, drop the clutch and feel the torque unleash its power through my tires into the C-trenches I had cut into the tract. My race has begun a fraction of a second before the rest of the riders waiting on the gate. It finally drops and the battle begins.

***

The gate dropping is just like someone pulling the trigger of a shot gun and I am the first piece of buckshot out of the barrel. My preplanning pays off and I have a wheel length jump in front of the other twenty-one racers at the start. Before we reach the end of the hole shot and right before the first turn I build the lead to half a bike length. So far so good, but there are twenty laps ahead and anything can happen.

The TV cameras are capturing the thousands of screaming fans in the stadium, the fans are being awed by the pyrotechnics surrounding the track that looks like a swarm of bees have just been unleashed on it and I am at the front of the swarm entering the first turn. It gets real dicey here. The track is wide enough to fit four or five bikes and riders, but there are twenty-two converging on it at the same time. Even though I got the jump I still have to be completely aware of all the riders right now. This is the big race and they are all pros as intent on winning as I am. Something's got to give. I nail the entry of the turn and rely on the bike to power through it. Willing every bit of power out of the machine I avoid the crowd of riders fighting for position in the bottleneck just behind me.

You have to be in more than just great physical shape in motocross. You have to be tough as well. It is a contact sport even at speeds in excess of fifty miles an hour. Every turn, jump and straight-away has the risks of riders making physical contact and sometimes the contact is very hard. In a crash, the dirt feels like concrete when you hit it and a motorcycle landing on you is no fun at all. No racer today will finish the race unscathed. There will be plenty of bruises and sprains. Hopefully no broken bones this time.

You also have to be able to keep a clear head. Every part of the track has its own unique hazards, but the turns are where most of the crashes take place. If the lead rider hits the brakes, everyone has to react in an instant. None of us like using the brakes, we all want to be full throttle all the time, but we have to control the bikes with finesse and we can also use the brakes to control the race. It's not always the fastest that keep the lead; it's often times the smartest. As the lead rider slows a little, you can bet that there will be other riders looking for a way around the leader. But when the lane to the lead is cut off they have to brake hard and they become an obstacle to riders coming up from behind. The ones who do not react in time become the first bike and rider of a pile-up.

The moment I clear the turn I have to maintain an intense focus on finding the rhythm that will keep me in the lead. Every muscle in my body is as taunt as piano wires holding on to the bike and man-handling it into the line. As I calculate exactly where I want to hit the first lip of the first jump I can hear the words of my trainer in the back of my mind. "Breathe, in your nose and out the mouth!" He screams. "You can't stay mentally sharp unless you breathe." It might sound strange that I have to remind myself to take a breath, but the adrenaline fuelled energy that my body is producing to maintain the clarity is crushing. Things are happening at lightning speed and I have to be ready to make adjustments in an instant all while focused on how to attack the track. I also have to be completely aware of the other riders. Even when they are behind me I can tell what is happening by the sounds of their bikes. It is a lot of information to calculate and, yes, sometimes I forget to breath.

I can feel some of them right behind me and one catching up to my right. I hit the first triple jump and it feels good. But I make a mental note to shoot for a different part of the lip next time around. In the air I get chance to steal a look around and see I was right. My lead now is only inches. When I awoke this morning I focused on the race. When it began, the laps. Now I have to dissect the laps into different parts of the track to find the most speed. I have to do all this while I have twenty-one other riders right on my back fender trying to figure out how and where to pass me.

I land the jump and go into the next turn a little high and am passed by another rider on the low side. I don't like it, but it's okay. I'll use him to find the line and pass him back up. I don't have the luxury of letting anything affect my concentration on the race. Not even losing the lead. As I leave the turn and pass through the next straight-a-way I get ready for the big jumps. In football, fans want seats on the fifty yard line. In motocross they want them right here, next to the jumps that send the riders the highest in the air. I hit the lip and it feels perfect. As I make the first big flight I get a millisecond to concentrate on concentrating. It's not a rest or a break, but the closest thing I will get in the next nineteen and a half laps. But I do use the hang time to plan any adjustments I have to make to win.

In the rest of the lap I begin to find the perfect rhythm and begin to feel in full control of the race. There are two other riders in the mix with me. In each turn we bang into each other fighting for the spot we each want to enter the straight-a-ways. We trade positions several times trying to find the best line to victory. A few bike lengths behind us, there is another group of four or five bikes then the rest of the pact pretty far behind them.

The first lap completed, I have all the information I need. The track talks to me and shows me where the line is. My bike and body are one as I settle into the rhythm and my mind is completely focused on milking every extra fraction of a second off my lap time. With bikes flying around me and the hard hits I am taking from bumping other riders in the turns in the next laps you would think it would be hard for me to keep my mind in the race. It's not. I'm in the zone. In the middle of all of this physically exhausting and mentally draining chaos I know exactly what I have to do. And I do it.

The only time I second guess myself is just after the halfway point in the race. In lap eleven or twelve I notice that the bike leaned a little harder in one of the turns than I wanted it to. I think to myself, "Is it my body, my focus, the bike?" For the last ten minutes, which feel more like hours, I have been in a full on, all encompassing sprint. No rest or breaks, just full throttle mentally and physically and I'm just half way there. This is where the true pros show their edge.

As I hit the big jump this time around I make a point to hit it a little higher which gives me a fraction more hang time. It cost me a fraction of a second, but I can use it to regain my concentration on controlling the rest of the race. It's still me and two other riders battling for the lead. One of the guys I know well, we have raced each other before many times. The other I never have shared a track with. He was one of the rookies who I heard was an up and comer in the sport. So far I am pretty impressed. With less than half the race to go it is becoming clear that it will be one of the three of us that will win. I decide it will be me. Then at the beginning of lap seven the rookie throws me a curve.

In motocross there is an understanding between riders. You do not try to win by making your opponents crash, plain and simple. It is not a courtesy. The race is too intense for that, just an unwritten rule. Someone forgot to tell this guy about it.

The three of us are still tightly grouped as we enter the first turn of the lap when the rookie tries to force me off the top of the curve. "What the...?" I think. Was it an accident or was this guy trying to take me out? He answered my question two turns later when he tried it again, only this time it was obvious. "Okay, you flipping idiot. My turn"

I let myself fall back a bike length as we enter the straight-a-way from the corner. I know this had to confuse the rookie. The first step of my plan is to throw him off his game a little. Even in the middle of the war I think of ways to damage the mindset of the other riders. As we set up for a small jump ahead I pull my bike into a wheelie and at full throttle take the jump. With him taking the jump at his regular pace and me using all the horsepower the bike can give, I pass him in the short air time and I get ready for the final attack. I take the next turn a little lower, forcing the rookie to take it high. Right at the moment we would use full throttle to get the best speed out of the turn, he does. I don't. Instead I tap my brakes. In the same instant I use the torque of the bike to twist it around a hair width. The rookie has no time to react as my back tire knocks into his front wheel causing it to twist against the line of the turn. By the time his lesson is learned I'm already setting up for the next big jump several bike lengths ahead, so I cannot see what happens. I don't have to, I already know. With his wheel out of control it becomes implanted in the wrong rut. Then phys-ics take over. The front wheel wants to stop, but the inertia of the bike has other ideas as the back end comes up. Now that the front wheel is dragging in the dirt the bike wants to slow, but the rider's body momentum wants to keep going. And it does. Right over the handlebars. The move that I use to teach him his lesson is so subtle in the roar of the race that it looks to the crowd that he just lost control, which he did with a little help from me.

With the rookie out of the picture I return my focus on the main goal, winning. The problem is that having to take care of business has cost me about ten bike lengths and I only have a couple of more laps to make it up. For some riders second place would be fine. Not for me. Time to turn it up a notch.

I'm sure scientists would say it is impossible, but I truly believe that great riders can use their mental energy to get more out of the bike than is physically possible. Whether it is the will to win or the refusal to accept defeat, it doesn't matter. All I know is that I have to win and have less than two laps to do it. I think the leader knows of my intentions also. I see him turning to look back at me in the jumps and sees that I am catching up. It's like he is a bleeding swimmer leaving a trace of blood in the water and I'm the great white, I can taste it. My focus and intensity makes up the time that was lost. The intimidation causes him to make the small mistakes that could cost him the race. I attack the turns more aggressively now feeling the G-force and praying that my tires keep their hold in the dirt. In the jumps I fly the bike flat to cut down on wind resistance, gaining that precious fraction of a second. Halfway into the last lap inches separate us. We both have to negotiate the obstacles of other riders we have lapped. I use those to my advantage, also. It's going to be close. The race officials place transponders on the bikes. The first electronic device to cross the finish line is the winner and both of our transponders are right next to each other.

Out of the last turn I can see the checkered flag. It's right there! I can also feel the other rider next to me. He's right there too. The crowd is screaming and the bikes are roaring as we both try to squeeze every last once of power out of the throttle. This time I really do stop breathing as I pass the finish line.

$$***$$

Minutes after the end of the race my body begins to feel every effect of the gauntlet and my adrenaline hangover is in full swing. It always amazes me just how much power and focus that quirky little hormone can give me. But the let-down after being amped up by it for hours can be brutal. Under the new bruises that are forming in my limbs there are reminders of some of the crashes I had in laps in the years past. The old surgeries and broken bones don't hurt. They are not even uncomfortable; they just remind me that they are there. The new bumps and scraps from the last race are not all that painful either. Just a low throb to let me know that they will be there for a while, too. Under the physical reminders, in my inner core, my body feels like I'm a Gumby after downing a handful of downers with a pint of Jack Daniels. I am exhausted. But my mind is recovering and is almost as sharp as when the gates dropped at the beginning of the race. I am regaining awareness of everything around me.

I have to laugh to myself about the first reward the officials give me when I win the big race. They take my bike away. The top three finishers have to surrender their motorcycles for one last check to ensure that they are within the allowed specs for the championship race. "Well, it keeps everyone honest," I think to myself. At least for the ones who don't get caught.

I do not feel cocky, but I have to tell you: It feels totally awesome to win. As long as I finish a race knowing that I gave it my best I feel good. No matter what position I come in. But, there is no substitute for being number one and all the work and mental torture has paid off big time today. I'm not quite done focusing yet. I won by less than a bike length. My mind is reliving every lap of the race I just finished to figure out how I could have won it by two, or three, or five, or ten… I have a lot more races in front of me and anything I can learn from this one will only build on all of my lessons from past races. I want to make sure I'm even harder to beat next time.

My team, friends and family are surrounding me making me feel like the most important person in the world. The space around us crackles with exuberance. I am grateful that we can share in the victory. It is one of the biggest highs a man can have. Seeing the excitement and joy in their eyes is as satisfying as winning the race. Well, almost.

Then I think of the rookie.

I ask Chad, "What happened to that guy who dumped his bike near the end of the race, did he finish?"

"No, he had to push his bike off the track, more like carry it. He buried his wheel in a rut and went over the handle bars. I don't think he was hurt but his bike got messed up pretty bad. The handle bars were toast."

"That sucks." I say, glad to hear he was okay. He was pretty good, and I am sure we will race each other in the future. I also know that he will think twice before he tries to take me out of a race again.

Chad looks at me through halfhearted accusing eyes and asks, "You wouldn't have anything thing to with his crash, would you?'

I say nothing.

He laughs, "You don't even feel guilty, do you?"

"About as guilty as a guy pulling the trigger in the middle of a duel," I say slyly.

In the following hour there was a bunch of picture taking and interviews and, of course, a ton of people come up to me to offer their congratulations. Now I can thoroughly enjoy the attention of the fans and sponsors. My mission has been accomplished. I won. The moment I enjoy most is when I hear over the loud speaker, "And in first place, Derek Costella!" It feels great, but I enjoy the crowds' roar even more.

When it's finally time to call it a day and head home, my wife and I are walking to the parking lot when one last reporter catches me. "Hey Derek, can I have just a couple of minutes?" Out of reflex I stop. I love my responsibility to the sport and I want to fulfill it. I tell Jackie that I'll catch up with her.

"I know this might sound like a dumb question, I'm just looking for a little filler. Do you name your bike?" The reporter blurts.

I think for a moment feeling my clowning around nature returning. "Yes, I do as a matter of fact!" I say with a false enthusiasm, trying to make him feel like he has asked the greatest question of the day. "I call it 'Bike.'"

He gives me an irritated look that says, "Alright, you got me." Aloud he says, "Okay, Okay. I know you're tired, but please, just one more quick question and then I'll leave you alone. I want to know what are you most afraid of out there on the track?"

I have been asked that question, or ones like it, hundreds of times over the years and I always I use my stock, joking around answers. For some reason I thought about it this time. Partly because I felt a little guilty for the "bike name" joke; the guy was just trying to do his job. Mainly I want to answer because I never thought about the question before. Not deeply. I am used to applying my energy to focus on winning the next race and being a better rider, not on what scares me. Maybe it is because I am completely wiped out and my defenses are down, but I want to give this guy the most honest answer that I can. After a few moments of reflection and to my chagrin I tell him, "Not finishing." He can tell I am being completely candid.

"Right." It is all he can say as he nods with understanding.

As I catch up to Jackie I think about the reporter's last question and my answer. It was the truth. "Not finishing" was and is my biggest fear, by far.

Then I slowly start to understand that things are not what I thought they were before. Not exactly. For years I have been confident that I had a crystal clear picture and complete control of every aspect of my career as a motocross racer. It has been a real source of pride for me and for the most part I have had both. But now a new picture becomes very clear in my mind. Some might call it an epiphany or some kind of Zen revelation, whatever. Now, for some reason that I can't explain, I get it. The race didn't start this morning for me when I first woke up. It started twenty years ago.

CHAPTER 2
ROOTS

I consider myself a successful motocross racer. I also have to tell you that I'm not all that special. I honestly believe anyone who is willing to fully commit to their dreams can achieve them, whatever they are.

On any given day I can be the best rider on the track, or not. It changes constantly and there are many top motocross riders I have the upmost respect for, even when they beat me. Although my main goal has always been and always will be to win, I have to understand there will be races where I congratulate someone for finishing ahead of me and I don't mind doing that at all. It truly is a sport of respect and they would do the same for me. I don't let it get to me as long as I know in my heart I gave it my all. But sometimes it takes a concentrated effort to maintain the mental focus on a day-to-day basis for doing the things I have to do to stay competitive. Especially after a loss.

Those closest to me would tell you that I have incredible discipline and an unusually high positive mental attitude, all the time. Maybe they're right, I never do something half-assed and I am always looking for ways to accomplish things and improve myself. I believe anyone can have this kind of mindset, although I also know many don't. I am no better or worse than anyone else. I share the same feelings, fears and desires that everyone does and I'm about as average as average gets. But I do have to admit that I have had one big advantage in being able to develop the character traits that have helped me succeed with my career in motocross. Being blessed with the most awesome, God loving, family in the world.

My family's from Felton, California, just north of Santa Cruz and about an hour's drive south of what is now known as the Silicon Valley. Tommy, my big brother, is fifteen years older than me and also into motocross. Bridget is my oldest sister and eight years older. My other sister, Nina, is three years my senior. As you can see, I am the baby of the family.

We were the fourth generation, on both mom and dad's side of the family, to live in the beautiful small town that was surrounded by Redwoods and was a little bit country. Everyone knew each other and I had a ton of aunts, uncles, and cousins that lived close to my home.

My dad owned his own excavation business and mom had a dress boutique, taught a ceramics class and worked at the local Christian school that all of us kids attended. We were not rich and we were not poor. We didn't have the designer labels on our clothes like some of the other kids, but we never wanted for anything and always had more than we needed. When it came to love and support, however, we were, by far, the wealthiest family in town. Maybe even the state.

A couple of years ago Nina got married and my family was there to celebrate. It was a great time as we all hung out and talked about times when we were growing up. The room was filled with love and laughter just like when we were kids as everyone shared their stories. I cringed when someone talked about some of my exploits as a kid.

Bridget loves to talk about the time the whole family went bungee jumping. I was a small kid and light as a feather. The first year I tried they wouldn't even let me on the jump platform. At sixty five pounds and the minimum being eighty five pounds I didn't have a chance. When my dad saw how disappointed I was he had a plan for the next year. This time, when I stepped on the scales for the weigh-in, he snuck up beside me and pulled down on my fingers so hard I heard my knuckles pop. He was trying to help me fool the scales and the jump masters. It worked. The scales tipped at the minimum weight. When it was my turn to jump everything went great until I reached the bottom of the rope length. I still didn't weigh enough to stretch the bungee rope, so I just stopped and hung like a dead fish. Some start for a daredevil... Both of my sisters laugh when they talk about the times I slowed them up when they went bike riding. I was a little kid who had to push his new bike up the hill trying with all his might to keep up with his big sisters screaming, "Wait for me, wait for me!" because I wouldn't let my dad put training wheels on it. I guess you could say I was a little stubborn. My family would say a lot. They all talk about how I could do any trick on my scooter when I was three that a teenager could do on a skateboard. The only time the laughter stops is when my mom talks about a couple of things that happened when I was far too young to remember.

Twice before I was a month old my lungs filled with fluids and paramedics had to rush me to the hospital to save my life. Obviously I made it, which shows that I was a fighter before I could even crawl, but it also makes me wonder. We all have that deepest spot of our brains that determines our innermost fears and how we deal with them. Some call it the "lizard part of the brain." It is responsible for self survival. I wonder that maybe the lack of oxygen might have burned up a couple of the cells in that part of my mind so things that would scare the heck out of most people are fun for me. The majority would be scared to death to try the stunts I do today. I find myself pushing myself now, just like when I was a kid, to expand the envelope more and more just to feel butterflies in my stomach.

When I was three I nearly drowned twice in one month. Both times my family was having one of our big family barbeques. I decided that I didn't need to wear the floaters that my mom had put on my arms, so I took them off and jumped into the pool. The problem was that I hadn't learned how to swim yet. Luckily my big brother jumped in and pulled me out of the water both times and took care of me as I coughed the water out of my lungs. Again that "lizard brain" thing crosses my mind as I hear my mother recalling the scary moments.

Mom and dad talk about how as a kid I loved to play on my dad's equipment from his construction business. It even caught the attention of one of the local newspapers, the "Santa Cruise Sentinel", which sent a reporter to check out the five-year-old who handled a tractor as well as the adults and carved out his own dirt BMX tracks. Unfortunately it never made it to the press. The interview was scheduled for October 17, 1989. The day of the devastating World Series earthquake.

Having a son as a motocross racer is not easy for a parent and mine started to see why before I even touched a motorcycle. I was a daredevil on a bicycle from the moment I figured out how to ride it. When the other kids started to ride in a straight line I was figuring out how to get the highest and farthest jumps out of my bicycle and how to build the best take-offs to make it happen. I was always getting hurt because I was never afraid to try something new. As I got older and started to ride BMX bikes the injuries increased in frequency and sometimes severity. I laugh to myself when I remember my dad bragging about me saying that I had great eye-hand coordination and the makings to be a top-notch athlete. If someone were to look at my medical records from when I was a kid, they might not agree. The people in the emergency room of our small town knew me on a first name basis because I was there so much. Among all the visits, I had to have stitches in my head seven different times before I was thirteen. I didn't suffer all the injuries because I was a klutz; it was because I was never afraid to push myself.

Our family was always together and very active. Camping, boating, skiing, you name it, we did it as a family. So my mom and dad already knew that I was adventurous at everything I tried when the subject of getting me a dirt-bike came up. At first my dad was against it. But, one day he came home from one of his jobsites with an old, beat-up Honda 50 for me. It was small, rusty, didn't run, and looked like it fell off a back of a truck. I loved it.

Dad was working a lot of late hours so he didn't have a chance to work on it right away. That didn't stop me from trying. For two weeks every day after school I would jump on its kick-starter trying to bring it to life for an hour at a time, bruising my thighs to the bone and blistering the arch my foot. It was only a couple of weeks, but it felt like months before my dad finally had the time to replace the spark plug and get some good gas in the tank. When he got it running for me I was in heaven. What a difference an engine makes! I rode it every chance I could. In the backyard, in front of the house and anywhere I could get away with it. If I could have taken it to bed with me, I would have.

It didn't take long for my parents to see that I needed a bigger and better bike. They remember thinking that I was a natural as I kept pushing the Honda 50 past its limits and nothing was going to stop me. On my tenth birthday I got the surprise of my young life. My brother and sisters still remember the look on my face when I first saw the shiny, new, yellow Suzuki DS 80 that my parents bought me. I literally came close to fainting. This bike had a suspension and came from the factory ready for the dirt. It was a quantum leap from the 50 and the only thing I hated was that it had a headlight and tail lights. Dirt bikes do not have lights so they had to go and they soon did.

Tommy had been riding dirt bikes for years, and he was good at it, so I had a coach right away with the bigger bike. He gave me pointers and my transition from the small Honda 50 to the DS-80, and what I believe was the start of my motocross career, was seamless. I caught on quickly how to control the bike and the extra power. I was tearing up the dirt in no time. My family owned a 55-acre parcel close to home. I was constantly riding on it improving my skills every chance I got.

In my youthful excitement as I jumped the new bike I thought I was catching some serious air. It was only a foot off the ground, but at the time I thought it was a big deal. So much so that I wanted to pass out flyers to the neighbors so they could watch me over the back yard fence. My first free-style event.

With the more powerful bike my parents again saw that I had a gift for the sport. I was able to do more with my bike than the other riders I rode with, but my bike was still smaller and not as well equipped as theirs. Also, I couldn't race in organized races and mom and dad saw that was what I wanted to do. So after a couple of years of begging and showing them I knew what I was doing when I was on the back of a motorcycle they got me a Kawasaki KX 60. It was twice the bike and I now had the opportunity to race for real. I could take this bike and go up against the big boys.

I won my first real race on the KX 60 and started to experiment doing tricks on it. I scared the hell out of myself, and I'm sure my family too, countless times. I pushed the bike to its limits and at the same time expanded mine. With the bigger bike I started to understand what I could do. I quickly learned how horsepower could be my friend or enemy. Respect it and you can use it to control the bike, disrespect it and the bike controls you. As I got better at handling the turns and became more confident with all the different aspects of riding I started to have fun thinking that I actually could be a real-life professional motocross racer, someday.

I do not have any kids, yet, but I do have an appreciation of what it must have been like for my parents. Motocross is a dangerous sport, plain and simple. Kids get hurt all the time and sometimes there are fatalities. Crashes, equipment failures and riders going the wrong way around the track are just some of the things that can get you hurt. When I first started racing, mom would keep her eyes closed most of the time except when I was passing by her on the track. I think mom and dad feared the "dirty riders" the most. Today in motocross there are plenty of times I have to watch out for the other rider who will cut me off or try to cause a crash, but when I was a kid, it was the worst. It was like some of the other riders went to kamikaze school and graduated with honors.

The closet track for real competition was at Hollister Hills, well over an hour away, but my parents made the time to take me there so I could compete. As much as they worried about my safety, they saw that I had potential and unselfishly encouraged my dreams to become a pro motocross racer. Most kids that age don't have a clue what they wanted to be when they grew up, I did, and the dream became clearer every day.

I won my first race on a bike that was the least powerful on the track; all the other bikes were modified, mine wasn't. It was purely my skill and determination that gained the victory. Soon I was getting some attention from others in the sport. But, because it was so far from home and the laws in the county were so restrictive of where I could ride I was limited on how much real practice I could get. Sometimes I would have to improvise and build my own track with my dad's construction equipment. It was never the same as the real races that were so far away. I didn't care what I had to do to get better and I loved every single moment when I was riding my motorcycle. My only limitation was gas.

Soon after the third bike upgrade, mom and dad had some news for the kids. We were moving. Everything was fine in Felton for us. Work was for good dad and everyone was happy, but my parents had decided that the family needed to take advantage of new opportunities. As far as work for my dad, there were other parts of the country that were booming and the money would be far better. They also felt that living in a bigger city might expand the kids' lives as well. So they told us that we were moving to a city in southern Nevada. Maybe you have heard of it, Las Vegas.

All the kids were super-excited because we knew we would meet new people and life in a big city would be completely different. We were also scared because life in a big city would be completely different.

As I look back at this time I realize how important my parents' decision to move was to my life as a motocross racer. As much as I loved living in Felton and being surrounded by family, it did have its limitations on how I could excel in the sport I had grown to love so much. I remember a bunch of riders from that time that should be pros by now, but the area was too restrictive to develop good motocross racers. In Las Vegas and at the age of thirteen I would be able to compete more and have access to many of the things that I would need to have a shot of turning pro. Most of those things simply were not available in Felton. It would also be easier on my parents to encourage and support me. The tracks were minutes away, instead of hours, and there were a lot more motocross resources in the city of lights.

I also look back and understand that the single-most important blessing I have had on my road to becoming motocross pro was, and is, my family. I am not a parent, but I have seen the result of a lot of parenting skills. Both good and bad. Mom and dad did more than just support me and encourage my dreams; they made sacrifices to help me achieve them. My brother and sisters along with many of my aunts, uncles and cousins were all there for me, also. In Felton, with the nearest real track being so far from home, it took a lot of help from everyone for me to get the limited experience I needed. If I didn't have that support when I was young I wouldn't be talking to you today as a professional racer. I'd be a riding my bike as a weekend warrior and watching the real races from the stands.

So, I guess you could say that being blessed by my family was a huge advantage for me when my lifelong race started at a very young age. It was like having racing fuel in my tank from the very start, so to speak. And, just like the last big race, when the gate went down on this one, I was already ahead. Only this time, I was way ahead.

CHAPTER 3
HEATING UP

"**R**eally!"

That was all I could think when I stepped out of the air-conditioned cab of the rental truck that hauled our family's household belongings from Felton to Las Vegas. It was mid-July and when we left my old home town it was eighty seven degrees. That was a super hot day for us. When my feet hit the steamy pavement in front of our new home in Vegas it felt like I was stepping into a furnace on steroids. When I asked my mom what the temperature was and she told me that it was one hundred and nine degrees. I thought to myself, "Well, this will take a little getting used to…" For those who say, "But, it's a dry heat," they are right, and it is still flipping hot.

My spirits were still high, though. As we pulled into the new neighborhood I saw mounds of dirt all over the place left behind by construction crews. Las Vegas was crushed by the economic down turn of 2008, but in 1996 it was a boom town. It was literally the fastest growing city in the United States and every area of free space was blooming with new neighborhoods. Our new home was located a couple of miles east of the famous strip; we could see the new mega resorts reaching for the sky as they were being built.

I couldn't wait. As soon as the truck door opened I pulled by BMX bicycle off the back and headed straight for the mounds of dirt that looked like they were put there just for me to jump. One thing I learned as a small kid — always take care of your equipment. To this day I clean and polish all my bikes and gear constantly, so my ride was gleaming. Its aluminum frame reflected the harsh Vegas sun and my anodized purple handle bars looked like they were brand new.

As my front wheel hit the base of the dirt pile my heart beat raced with excitement and then skipped a beat. In Felton the dirt was hard-packed and my tires always easily rode on top of the surface. In Vegas it is much sandier, so instead of going up the mound, my front tire plowed itself into the soft sand sending me over the handle bars and onto the steep decline on the other side of the slope. As I slid down I was engulfed in a cloud of dust so thick I couldn't see an inch in front of me. When I got up I looked down at my clothes. My blue shorts and red t-shirt were now the same color and it looked like they were dusted in powered sugar. When I picked up my bike I couldn't see what color it was, either, it looked just as dirty as me.

When my mom saw me pushing my bike onto the driveway, she laughed. I looked into the rear view mirror of the truck and saw what she had found so amusing; the only part of the reflection that didn't show the dust was my eyes. Every other part of me was completely covered and I looked like I was wearing some kind of freakish Halloween costume dressed up as a leaking jelly-filled doughnut, the jelly being the blood dripping from my elbows and knees. It hurt, but I had to laugh, too. It was pretty funny, but unfortunately it was also a precursor of what I would go through on the tracks when I started up motocross racing in Nevada.

In our first months in Vegas as we settled in I didn't ride my motorcycle often. I had gone through a growth spurt, and my KX 60 was still fun to ride, but it wasn't a challenge anymore because it was too small for me. Instead I spent a lot of time on my BMX bike. Having a dad who owned excavation equipment was a huge plus — I was able to build awesome BMX jumps across the street from my house. I also had two hundred feet of water hose running to it so I could keep the dirt tapped down. I had learned my dusty lesson from my first stab at the Vegas soil. It was fun on the BMX bike, but in my heart I still wished I was using a throttle instead of pedals. I was getting tired of banging up my shins with the pedals and I missed the challenges of motocross.

Mom and dad still were not completely sold on the idea of me racing motorcycles when I was thirteen and money was a little tight after the expense of the move. Buying me a new bike was not on the list of priorities. I still kept in the loop and always sought information about the races and racers. I found out that, as far as motocross was concerned, we had moved to a different planet.

The sport was taken far more seriously here and the competition was off the charts compared to what I was used to back in Felton. We would go check out the Las Vegas Motor Speedway in North Las Vegas and watch the races. The lap times were incredibly fast and the intensity of the races could have intimidated me, but I didn't let it. Instead I started to set my goals. At the time I had no idea how, but I was determined to be in those races and to win. I also later learned that the real action for the sport was in Southern California. It was to motocross what the North Shore of Oahu was to surfers. I started to picture myself racing there, also.

There are many levels of competition. The amateur group is comprised of Beginner, Novice and Intermediate levels. In these events the only tangible rewards are trophies. There is also the Amateurs-Pro where you can make a few bucks, but it is nowhere near what it's like when you hit the big time. There are also categories for age groups. I quickly understood that if I had a shot of qualifying in any of these groups I was going to have to get a better bike. I also understood that I would have to whip my butt into shape. After seeing the beating these racers were taking, it was a no-brainer. I became so obsessed with my dream that it started to affect other parts of my life. I became a fierce competitor in anything I did: video games, sports at school. Anything at all where someone would win and someone would lose I did everything I had to do to be the winner.

I spent my free time working with my dad. I used his equipment to dig the deep holes for new pools and other type of excavation work. It was funny when someone new first saw me work the equipment. They would always say, "Hey, that kid can't be doing that, he's way too young!!" I guess they didn't expect a thirteen-year-old to be running a tractor. Dad would always tell them to just watch me awhile and within a few minutes they could see I was just as good as any of the adults.

One afternoon while on one of dad's worksites he called me over to a rock pile and handed me a huge sledge-hammer. I had been constantly asking him about getting a new motocross bike for months. He pointed to a very large piece of concrete and said, "One swing. If you can break it, we'll talk about a new motorcycle…" I have never been big, and the tool felt like it weighed a ton in my hands, but I wanted the newer and bigger bike so much I didn't care if I put myself in the hospital trying to break the stupid stone. I lifted the hammer and moved it over my shoulders so both of my hands could have a good hold as I swung it over my head and slammed it onto the stone. When it hit with a loud "crack" the hammer jumped off the concrete and I felt the shock rattle all through my body, but the concrete stone was still intact. I couldn't believe it; I had never hit something so hard in my life. I knelt down and brushed off the dust that exposed a crack running down the middle of the stone. "Dad, dad, dad, look I did it!" He came over and checked out the crack and shook his head. It must have been enough; I had my new Honda CR80 a couple of days later.

The new motorcycle was a little big for me and therefore challenging, but I loved it. I would ride it in the concrete-walled washes used for flood control that laced through the neighborhoods and under the streets out to the desert where I could practice to my heart's content. Sometimes people would call the cops because of the dust clouds I was making, but I never got caught. I would just race back home in the washes if they showed up. The real fun was when I started to hit the track.

Motocross racing didn't come naturally to me; I had to work hard at it and the level of competition was a quantum leap from what I was used to at Felton. As I started racing at the Las Vegas Motor Speedway I found out who the fastest riders were and made a point to set my goals to be better than them. I also loved every minute being on the track; it blew the doors off messing around out in the desert.

Between fourteen and sixteen I competed in more than a hundred races throughout Utah, Southern California and Vegas and had earned a reputation of being one of the best riders early on. But when I first started I had some troubles. The jumps never caused me any problems, but I would crash way too often in the turns. It would frustrate me to no end. Not only did it add to my lap times, it hurt! In one of my earlier races I was in the last lap and firmly in the lead. I knew that I was going to get the first place trophy, but in the last turn I dumped my bike. I remember being so angry about the crash that I picked up my bike and tried to push into the second place rider as he passed me. I missed, luckily, but I was still in a rage. When I got back to the pits I slammed my helmet on my knee then started to kick my dad's truck bumper. A couple of hours later my leg started to hurt and I was feeling embarrassed about my tantrum. I learned right then and there not to let myself get angry. It was a complete waste of energy that I could be using to improve myself instead of looking like a fool. But, I was still having trouble with the turns.

Like I said before, my parents have always supported me in the pursuit of my dreams, but after they saw my commitment to the sport when I started to race in Vegas, they took it to a new level. I remember my dad telling a friend not long ago about how hard it was at first. It was time-consuming, frightening and very expensive. But after seeing what I was willing to do my mom and dad became as committed to me becoming a professional motocross racer as me. I heard my dad say, "We had to, there was no way we could not help him when he was willing to pay such a big price on his own…"

So dad found a school in Cedar City specializing in motocross. Yes, there really is a school for motocross racers. With the travel and cost of the seven-day school it was expensive, but dad did get me there for one day. That's all it took. I was taught by one of the top riders in the country. He showed me that just by turning my head the wrong way to see who was on my tail or to check out the dirt rooster shooting up from my back tire was enough to make me crash. Then the entire day was spent learning different techniques and tricks of the trade. When the other riders took a break for lunch, I was on the track reinforcing what I had learned. I think the instructor saw how committed I was and knew my family's financial resources were low, so he gave me some individualized attention. I gained more knowledge in that one day than six months on the track. It was also cool that we got to watch the instructor race that night. He won. I came in third in my race and I nailed every turn.

Anyone who is truly serious about being a rider in motocross has a lot of things to focus on. Being in great shape and keeping the equipment in order are important, but for me the most important thing I can do is to set goals. I concentrate so much on what I want to achieve that after a short time thinking about my goal, I can already feel it like it has happened. Some might call me obsessive, but I believe that goal-setting gives me an edge.

When I started to race in Vegas I made sure that I only compared myself to the best riders. They all had much more experience on the track than me, but I knew that if they could do it, I could too. When you combine the habit of setting goals, a healthy spirit of competition and being willing to put your heart into it, then you have the core materials you need to be a pro.

I quickly became known as one of the fastest riders in Las Vegas and started to win so many trophies that I stopped saving them. Instead, I would take off and save the plates with my name, place, and name of the race. As I got better it also became more expensive for my family. There are a lot of costs with this crazy sport. There is a lot more than the investment in the bike and fuel. There are a ton of fees that have to be paid to compete, travel expenses and too many miscellaneous cost factors to list. It was getting harder and harder on my parents to foot the bill, so we started to look for sponsors.

My first sponsor was Red Carpet Kawasaki-Suzuki-Honda. It was a small shop in Vegas that gave us some nice discounts on the equipment. It wasn't a big time deal, but every little bit helped. The owner liked my family and was always willing to help out the best that he could. One day he surprised me. There was another family with a kid racing in my class that shopped there also. The owner didn't like the dad very much; I guess they got into it a couple of times. The owner told me that if I beat the other kid at Golden State Nationals I could have my pick of anything in the shop. When I blew the other kid away and ended up with a two-hundred-and-twenty-dollar FOX jacket I was pretty stoked, even though I wasn't into leather and it was too big for me. He gave me another chance and after I beat the other rider for a second time I made a better choice — a three-hundred-dollar Shoei helmet.

My next sponsor was a bigger deal. It had two companies, "909" and "FMF," both of which manufactured and sold after-market parts for motorcycles and apparel. It is still one of my sponsors to this day, but at the beginning the contribution "909" and "FMF" just put a dent in the cost of my racing. Again, every little bit helped. But if I was going to be able to go pro it became painfully clear that I would have to get some big time sponsors and the only way that was going to happen was for me to keep on pushing the envelope and winning races.

I kept hearing about how things in Southern California were much different than Vegas. The tracks were a lot more difficult and some of the best riders in the world lived there. I realized that if I was going to have a shot at going pro I was going to have to start to race in that part of the country. That was where the big races and sponsors were. At first I was a little nervous. I was becoming one of the kings of the track in Vegas; thinking about having to prove myself all over again against better riders, some of which were national champions, was something I had to prepare myself for. I was becoming addicted to winning and the thought of starting over again was unsettling.

In some ways it wasn't that far from Vegas, but in other ways the three-hundred mile-drive was a true journey. Dad still had his business to run, so driving back and forth every other weekend was hard, and it was also another cost to drain the bank account.

As we started to make the trek to Southern California we also got introduced to the motocross subculture. The things that the fans never see. In the pits there are several travel trailers, our temporary homes, and a small community springs up. There are the parents and family members that are only there to support their rider and they bring the competition and their negative attitude from the track to the pits. But, For the most part, there is a strong social bond that exists between the rest of the families. There was nothing that our friends would not do for us and nothing that we wouldn't do for them. Sometimes it was simple, like loaning tools or first aid kits, sometimes it was more important, like letting another rider use a bike because his broke down. We shared meals and every victory and loss together. Strong friendships were formed. In fact many of the people we have been blessed to meet at the races over the years are still good friends of our family to this day. It takes a special type of family to be able to handle the pressures that come with supporting the racers and as far as I am concerned motocross have some of the greatest people in the world working behind the scenes. They never get a chance for the glory like the riders and sometimes the only reward they will have is being broke, but you will not find a kinder bunch anywhere.

The California tracks were brutal. I had been exposed to different types of tracks before. The track in Vegas was always groomed and smooth. It seemed like the only way to compete was to twist the throttle; it was almost like racing on a street. Utah's red dirt was real soft and took a little more finesse to get the most out of the track and the best lap time. Even riding in the deserts around Vegas had taught me a lot. But I understood why the reputation of Southern California's tracks and riders was so foreboding after my first lap.

At the track in Vegas I could go a lap without hitting a deep rut; in California I would be lucky to make it a yard. After one lap I was more exhausted than I would be after an entire race back home. The track literally beats on your body and shakes it to the core. It also tries to destroy your bike. Before, I would often tell people that a race felt like a roller coaster with the jumps and the g-forces I could pull in the turns. But it was fairly smooth. Now in California it still felt like a roller coaster, but the cars had square wheels and someone put speed bumps every ten feet on the tracks. They were truly jarring.

Up to this point, the only thing I needed to focus on was speed, but now I had to respect the track and figure out how to get the best speed while staying in control of the bike. I also learned how I could use the track to my advantage to out-maneuver the other riders. I guess you can say that I was introduced to the "line," the groove in the track I mentioned before that leads to the fastest lap times, on the California tracks. And then there were the California racers. These guys were racing on a different level. The lap times were super fast, even though they had to navigate some of the toughest tracks in the world. And there were more of them. I was used to having to race with seven to twelve racers at a time. Here there were as many as forty on the track at the same time and I had to learn how to deal with racing among the masses. The turns were more intense and the jumps were crazy compared to what I was used to. I caught on fast and was quickly moving up the ranks.

By this time I had gone through some bikes, but now had two, my Kawasaki KX 80 and KX 100, so I could compete in the fourteen-to-sixteen-year-old classes and the super-mini class. Even with the extra time on the track, I still wanted more. My family remembers hearing the announcer's voice over the loud speaker during some of the qualifying rounds where I was not competing calling out my name, "And you can hear Derek Costella out practicing!" He was right; after I finished my races I would go to the other track and hone my skills while the other races were still underway.

I still laugh when I remember how we got the money for the bigger bike. I started to put in some good lap times and even won a couple of races in California. The father of one of the other racers was convinced that my bike was over-powered and that was the only reason why I was doing so well on the track. My dad and I tried to explain that the bike was actually a little less powerful than most of the other bikes on the track, but the guy wouldn't listen. He offered my dad way more than the bike was worth and dad took the deal. We had the money for the bigger bike. I think God was helping me out with that one.

As my seventeenth birthday got nearer the pressure to find sponsors increased, big time. Soon I would be too old to be competing in the classes I was racing in and the cost of competing at the next level was staggering. My entire family was confident I had the skills and the proven record to be sponsored. The challenge was to get noticed. My dad went to everyone he could find in the industry and finally hit pay dirt when he talked to the manager for Kawasaki's Amateur team and convinced him to come check out one of my races. If he liked what he saw in me on the track, it would have been a huge deal for us. The bikes would be paid for and the financial support would make it possible to get to the next level and beyond. Win or lose, when he came out to see me it would be the single-most important race of my life.

When we got word that the manager was coming to check me out everyone in my family and our close circle of friends in the pits became giddy. It was a victory for all of us and the night before the race you could feel the happiness in the air. The dream was becoming a reality. It was easier for all of us to laugh and impossible not to smile. It felt like we had finally made it and the first big step to the main goal — becoming a professional motocross racer — was at hand. My dad and I decided to get to bed early and as we walked back to the trailer everyone was slapping our backs and wishing us luck.

The next morning everything checked out fine. The bike was ready and I had walked the track and felt confident I could master it. I remember feeling different before this race. The stakes were much higher. There were still the other racers and the crowd of fans, but knowing that how I did in this race might determine when I got sponsored was surreal for me. I never doubted that I would get sponsored. I did worry about how long it might take. I wasn't nervous or over-confident, just thankful to have the opportunity to show what I could do on the track. We lined up the bikes, the gates dropped and I started the race of my life.

I nailed every turn and everything went perfectly. I was in complete control and riding better than ever before, until the fifth lap. To this day I can't explain what happened. I was in the lead and knew I could win the race when, in an instant, I was on the ground and unable to move. I still cannot remember what caused the crash, but it was bad. Very bad. I had crashed many times before and would always get back up on the bike and keep on racing, still winning many times. But this time it was different. I had never been in so much pain before and for the first time I wasn't sure what to do. My body was numb and hurting at the same time and my arms and legs wouldn't move no matter how hard I tried. For the first time on the track I was scared as I heard the other racers buzz by me and it felt like I was lying on the dirt for an eternity.

"I got you, son."

It was all I could hear him say as my dad lifted me from the dirt and started to carry me off the track. I never had to be helped off the track before and having to be carried off should have bothered me, but it didn't. In my mind the crowd and other riders weren't there. I was way too out of it. I felt like I was in another dimension where everything had slowed down to a crawl. Everything except for the tears I could see running down my dad's cheeks.

It took me a while to gather my thoughts after we got back to the pits. I could feel the atmosphere and how much it had changed from the night before. The sorrow was too immense to ignore. After I had a chance to regain my senses, I got it. All the sacrifices and commitments by me, my family and friends over the years could not change things. I understood that in an instant my professional motocross career may have ended before it even had a chance to begin.

CHAPTER 4
PERCEPTIONS

A while after my crash I was interviewed by one of the bigger trade magazines and asked, "Why are you not sponsored when you are beating some of the biggest-sponsored racers out there?"

That had been *the* question for my family and me for some time. In order to understand the whys, you first have to understand how the sponsors work. Just like the different classes of motocross races, there are many levels of sponsorship. For those of you who think there is a lot of money in the sport, I have some good news and I have some bad news. The good news is that you are right; there is a lot of money in the sport. The bad news is that most of it comes out of the racers and their families' pockets, at least at the start.

First are those small-time sponsors who want you to put stickers advertising their stuff on your helmet and they won't charge you for the sticker. Not a whole lot of help in the big scheme of things. The first real step is usually from local businesses and mostly motorcycle shops. Many of these are small firms and the owners can't afford to put too much into to it. Instead they offer discounts on parts. For someone starting out it can be a big help. Buying the bike is just the beginning of the money that has to be put out to race. The bikes have to be modified and there are always parts that have to be replaced. You can spend as much as the bike costs every couple of months if you're racing a lot, things break all the time. It's a win-win situation. The business owner gets his name in front of the crowds at the track, so when junior tells dad that he wants motocross stuff he already knows where to send him. The shop does not have to put out hard cash, just lose out on part of the profit from the markup on the merchandise they would be selling anyway. For the riders the discounts help. Getting a better deal on tires, parts and sometimes bikes stretches the budget. But the cost to compete is still very high and usually has to be picked up by the rider, or more accurately, the rider's parents.

There are also companies that manufacture after-market parts for motocross —mostly parts to improve the bike performance. Wheels, handlebars, cables, sprockets, tires, you name the part of a bike and there is a huge chance that someone makes a better version than the stock part. To be competitive you need these and they are expensive. There are also companies that sell other gear, like clothing and helmets. They often provide their goods at discounts or for no charge. Many times they will offer incentives. Win a big race using their product and a nice cash bonus may be the reward. Although getting the parts at no cost can be an advantage for a racer, there are still plenty of other things to spend a ton of money on.

The next level is where things start to get interesting. There are very few solo racers who get lucrative deals. The vast majority of the big money from the big sponsors goes to teams and many of these teams are sponsored by the manufactures of the motorcycles. Once you hit this level the rewards are high and so is the pressure. Now you get bikes and everything you need to be hard-to-beat on the track and they are provided to you at no cost. Totaled your bike last night in a bad jump? No problem, a new one will be delivered to you today. Tires a little worn? They replace them, no questions asked. Need a little money for a hotel while you're on the road? Sorry, you're on your own. The only sponsor who can provide free bikes are the manufactures, but the rider still has to foot his own travel expenses as well as many other costs. And you have to perform well to stay on the team.

You know you hit the big time when you get sponsored by a company that foots the entire bill and pays you to race. Most other sports have companies that have nothing to do with the sport, but provide big money to get their name out. I don't think that Viagra has a lot to do with NASCAR and most golfers don't care what watch they are wearing when they are teeing off. In motocross the vast majority of the companies that put money into the sport are directly involved with it in one way or another. But there are exceptions. There have been a couple of major car and truck companies that pay big money to top racers and also provide free cars. Energy drinks pour a lot of money into the sport also, no pun intended. With this type of sponsorship a rider can actually make a comfortable living off the sport and it is the dream of every racer. And it is a real business. There are agents that pair up riders and sponsors just like actors and singers in the entertainment industry. Their job is to get the best deal possible for the rider.

Here is where it gets confusing. You would think that getting a sponsor would be easy. Just win all the time and they will be knocking your door down to sign you up, right? Wrong. A lot more is involved with the process. You have to be able to sell yourself to the right people to have a shot at the big time. Before the economic crash of 2008 I saw plenty of riders who were not the best ones on the track get good deals.

Although it is important to be consistently finishing in the top spots to have a shot at getting the company's attention so they will open up their checkbooks for you, there are politics also. Are you likeable? Can your face sell more product? Is there a "problem" with your past? There are so many aspects of how the process works that it can be mind-boggling at times and make you thankful to have an agent to navigate the mine field for you.

This is just a brief overview of the business aspect of motocross; there are many more facets. Over the last ten years I have lived most of them, but at the age of sixteen I didn't grasp the complexity of the game. I just wanted to race and win. The rest was an afterthought. Now at twenty-eight I have a much deeper appreciation of the business of the sport. I now know what it feels like to support my wife, have to pay a mortgage and manage my bills. I am often asked for advice by young riders about how they should pursue their careers. I'm honest with them. I tell them if they truly love the sport and are in it to win, go for it and do not let anything hold them back. I also tell them that if they are in it for the money, get out of racing now, take about half of what they would spend on motocross and go to law school and make the big bucks after they graduate. That way they might be able to afford helping their kids if they decide to go into motocross. I know it may sound funny, but the riders who make the most, care the least about the money. It's the love of racing that provides their motivation. The ones who are in it for the money don't last long and never win.

Although I may not have had a real concern about the money when I was almost seventeen, my dad did. He had to. It was getting too expensive for him and the pressure was building. As strange as it may sound, I'm thankful that I didn't fully understand the money part of racing back then. If I had, it might have taken away part of my drive and held me back from accomplishing what I have. If I had not accomplished those things I may never have gotten the sponsors over the years. It wasn't easy, but I can tell you that for me it was worth it. It took a lot of hard work and a little luck. Okay, a lot of luck.

I still think back to when I crashed when the team manager of the Kawasaki team came to the race to check me out when I was sixteen. I know a lot of people would have quit and there would have been no shame. Mom and dad might have had some extra money to take a vacation and I would have found work and rode my bike on the weekends. Everything would have been cool. But, the thought never crossed my mind. In my youthful, ignorant bliss I only had one thing on my mind.

"I have to get back on the bike…"

And I did, with a vengeance. I remember when I was younger I never understood how people could tell me that having something bad happen to them turned into one of their biggest blessings. Maybe it was a close call on the freeway or finding out there was something wrong physically. They would explain to me that they had a new appreciation of life and all it had to offer. They realized that taking risks was the only way to enjoy life to the fullest. After my bad crash when I was hoping to get noticed by the sponsor, I could understand where they were coming from. It took me a while, but I saw that the only person holding me back was me. The crash was the worst thing that could have happened, short of getting crippled or killed, and I survived it.

It changed my perspective. I have always been aggressive on the track, but after tasting the worst, my eyes were opened to see how I could achieve the best.

There are plenty of great riders out there and sometimes the only thing that makes them better is that they are willing to push harder than everyone else, no matter what the risk. I had been the guy who would take it to the limit, or at least what I thought was the limit. The realization that the little fears I had were holding me back turned out to be one of the most important lessons of my professional life. Don't get me wrong, I did not develop a death wish, but I did begin to clearly understand that if I was going to make it to the top I had to blow the doors off my comfort level.

Being one of the best was no longer an option; I had to be the top rider. I also understood that no one wins all the time, but I couldn't let myself off the hook with that. Even if I won and didn't give it a hundred percent, I still lost. If I lost and knew in my heart of hearts that I did give it my all, I was the biggest winner on the track no matter what place I came in.

As I tried to explain this to my friends and family, they thought I was nuts. I was already pushing the "radical" envelope more than anyone they knew. But I saw the bigger picture. It wasn't a matter of doing what I wanted to do; it was a matter of doing what I had to do to be the best. I guess that's why they call motocross an extreme sport; you have to be willing to be extreme to have a chance of winning.

The crash was humiliating. No one likes to screw up in front of a crowd, let alone have their dad carry them off the track. It was painful; I had never hurt so much. I used the experience to change the way I looked at things and therefore the way I did things to be more competitive. The biggest improvement, I feel, is that it took away the fear. I rationalized that if I got hurt, the doctors could fix me. That "lizard brain" deal in a way. They can grow back a tail and the docs could put me back together. People get killed in motocross. I said to myself, "Well if God wants to take me, I'm his anyway."

Looking back now I understand why my parents were unnerved. The ever-present financial pressure would have been enough. Now having their almost seventeen year old son tell them that he was going to take more big risks after they thought that was what was going on in the first place, well my mom deserves medal...

With my new perspective I didn't let the fact that I wasn't sponsored get to me anymore. Instead I decided to do whatever it took to get sponsored, so I searched out every rider that was sponsored by Suzuki and made sure to beat them on my Suzuki. When we were on the track and they were letting off the throttle, I was gunning it. If they jumped high, I jumped higher. When I crashed, which wasn't very often, I wouldn't let it bring me down. I would get back on the bike with new lessons learned and my comfort zone stretched out a bit more, making me harder to beat.

I also made a point to learn from my competition. Before I would never admit that there might be someone better out there than me. Now I not only admitted it, I embraced it and made a point to observe their superior techniques and implemented them into my own riding. Even in the pits I became more willing to learn. Before when someone would try to give me advice I would almost resent it, it felt insulting to me. In my young mind I thought I should have been the one dealing out advice. Now I understood that no one knows everything and when someone who knows what they are talking about shares information it can be a very valuable tool to make you faster on the track.

As I look back, I find it ironic that a crash that could have ended things for me turned out to be a launching point instead. Over the next several years I would accomplish a lot in the sport for many reasons. With a new openness and willingness to learn I did become a much better rider. Taking the lid off any and all fears gave me the intensity I would need to be a pro. I was blessed to have some incredible people come into my life and yes, sometimes I got lucky. But the new attitude, or at least the amped-up version of my old one, gave me an edge that I didn't have before and allowed me to take full advantage of the other aspects of my career. The old adage, "take lemons and make lemonade," might apply here, but I think it went deeper for me. Before the crash I was thinking like an amateur, a good one, but still green. Now I was thinking like a pro even though I wasn't in that class yet and that made all the difference in the world.

CHAPTER 5
THE HEALER

I had far too many bumps, bruises and sprains to count when I had what I consider to be my first big crash when my dad had to carry me off the track. Actually, I wasn't seriously hurt, just in a state of shock. My left side felt like it had been hit by a truck and my leg turned an ugly purplish-blue from my butt to my calf the next day, but overall I was feeling okay within a few days. I was back on my motorcycle right away and, with my new intensity level, feeling invincible. Some might call it the "Superman" syndrome, but I did feel like I could handle anything mentally or physically as long as I was willing to take out all fear and not hold back, not even a little bit. It was my new mindset and it felt good, in fact it felt great, and my confidence level went through the roof right away. Unfortunately, my body has had to pay a pretty big price for that confidence.

You do not have to be a diehard fan of motocross to understand that the risks for injury are incredibly high. In fact it is assured that if you race for any amount of time at the professional level you are going to get hurt. Guaranteed. There may be some pro rider out there who has never suffered a serious injury during his career, but I never met or even heard of him. With speeds in excess of fifty miles an hour and jumps that can be as high as fifty feet in the air, the chances of crashing are always there and always unexpected. One moment everything is fine, the next you're wondering if you are going to need surgery to put you back together. The safety equipment is minimal. Of course there are the helmets, but other than that there is rarely more between you and the chance for disaster than a nylon jersey or maybe a quarter inch of rubber on the heels for your boots. In other sports there are pads for every part of the body to absorb sudden shocks and to protect the skin from being ripped off. Not in motocross.

There are things you can do to reduce the risks and the most important is to stay in great physical shape. Riders are more like the wiry type of athletes, not the pumped-up linebacker versions you watch on Monday night football. Although pro motocross riders are extremely strong for their size — they have to be to control the bike and even stay on it in the first place — they also want to stay as light as possible. Every extra pound takes away from lap times whether they are on the bike or the rider. The equation is eight pounds equals a horsepower. So, motocross is not a big man sport.

The most important part of being in shape is in the cardio department. I constantly wear a heart rate monitor. The goal is to get my heart pumping as fast as possible. If I can hit one hundred and ninety beats per minute and keep it there for forty or fifty minutes, I'm doing well. The problem is that the better shape you are in the harder it is to keep the heart rate up. It is easy for a couch potato to get his heart pumping faster, which usually happens after a couple of flights of stairs. But for someone who is in good shape it takes more. As the function of the lungs and heart improve it takes a great deal more physical effort to elevate the heart rate, but the rewards are powerful. When you are in good shape you have a much sharper mental focus, so the chances of getting hurt from a stupid mistake go down dramatically. You also heal faster when the mental focus is not enough to avoid the injury. I learned this the hard way not long after my life-changing crash.

It had been a rainy week in Vegas, which is rare, and the dirt on the track became a sloppy mess. I was sure no one would have been doing laps in the miserable weather when I went out to take a practice run after the sky cleared. I was wrong. Someone had taken their four wheel drive off-road truck around the track a few times and cut huge scaring ruts into the track. I didn't do my usual walk around; I was too excited to get in some practice after the down time. So I hopped on my bike and gunned it. When I cleared the first turn I didn't see the damage to the track in time and my front wheel crossed up and planted firmly in the gouge. My left shoulder took every bit of the energy of the crash as my bike instantly went from forty plus miles an hour to zero. I could hear a loud, sickening popping sound as my joint was dislodged from its socket. I never ever knew pain like this before. It felt like a monster had literally tried to rip my arm off and almost succeeded. Luckily one of my buddies was with me, so he rode back to my house and got my dad who took me to the hospital. The wait in the emergency room was the longest of my life. Three full hours with no pain medicine as my shoulder felt like it was exploding.

When I was finally examined by the doctors they found that not only was my shoulder dislocated, I had also had a fracture in my shoulder blade. The pain killers were a welcome relief as I heard the doctors tell my dad that they were going to sedate me before popping my shoulder back into place. I still remember the feeling of going under the chemical haze as I heard the doctor telling my dad, "We need you to leave the room now. You *do not* want to hear this sound…" I thought as I drifted off, "If it sounds the same popping in as it did popping out, I don't want my dad to hear it, either."

When I woke up the flaming pain had calmed to a low-roaring throb, but I felt whole again. The doctor's orders were rest and stay off the bike for a couple of months to give my body a chance to heal. I was back on the track in a few weeks.

I guess you can say that my right shoulder was a little jealous of all the attention that my left one was getting, because less than a year later I dislocated it also during a race in California. Right out of the gate another rider took me out by sliding his back tire into my front wheel causing it to wash out. We were going super fast and the stopping force was instantaneous. Just like before, the joint took the full impact, this time it was on the other side.

I learned how important it is to have competent medical attention because this time things did not go as smoothly. I was rushed to the emergency room like before, but this time the doctor decided that he would pop my shoulder back into place without putting me under. Also, like before, my father was told to leave the room while the procedure was taking place and he did. He was back at my side the instant he heard my screams. The doctor had wrapped a sheet around my torso and another sheet around the dislocated arm. He had the nurse hold the first sheet as the doctor pulled on the other sheet, trying to get my shoulder to pop back into place. I'm not sure if there were complications or if the doctor was just making mistakes, but I knew the pain I was going through couldn't be right and something was going terribly wrong. I tried not to scream, but the intensity of the pain and the fear ripped through my entire body and I was completely out of control. I could actually feel the bones fighting each other while grinding, resisting all the doctor's attempts to get the joint back into its socket.

I looked up and saw the fear in my dad's eyes and it intensi-fied my horror to a point where I thought I would be thrown into a full stage panic. After what seemed like hours, but was most likely only a few moments, we all heard the horrible pop-ping sound as my right shoulder finally found its place. This time there was not the relief I felt before in Vegas. I could tell that something was wrong and my dad finally convinced him to take more x-rays. After reviewing the ghostly white pictures from before and after my so-called treatment it was evident that the doctor had fractured my shoulder while trying to get it back into place.

Now, instead of just having to deal with the pain, my dad and I were forced to deal with the doctor's mistakes and the emotional rage was hard to control for both of us. Dad took me home to Vegas and this time my recovery time was much longer. I also had a new impression of my dad; I have never seen him so angry. The doctor called him for several days to see how I was doing. I'm not sure if he was genuinely concerned for my well being or if he was worried about the potential lawsuit, but his follow-up care blew the doors off his medical technique.

One of my most frustrating injuries happened when I was eighteen and had achieved a degree of success in the sport. I had gotten some great sponsors and a big part of the financial load was taken off my parents. It felt good to hand over checks to them after all the years they sacrificed helping me pursue my dreams. It helped pay the travel expense and entry fees.

I had a mechanic before Chad who had a great reputation in the sport and had done a fine job for me. The bikes were always operating in top notch condition every time he handed them over before the races and we were winning. I was competing in the Amateur Nationals in California and was in fifth place overall when we were heading into the last race. My confidence level was as high as ever and I believed I could bring home the first place trophy. Then the gates dropped. I could tell right away that there was something wrong. The bike not only didn't feel right, but felt like it was completely off balance. There are so many things that can go wrong with motocross motorcycles; it's not just about horsepower and weight. The suspension is critical. If it is dialed in right, the rider remains in complete control in the turns and the roughest part of the track, especially the bumps that fill the straight-a-ways. If it is not adjusted properly the bike becomes difficult to control. This time the bike was completely out of whack. In the first turn I had a hard time staying on the track, let alone on the line.

Then came the "woops," a series of small jumps that have to be hit precisely to have any chance of winning the race. I tried to put the thought that something was wrong with the bike out of my mind and focus on getting the best lap times. I pushed it harder thinking that I could compensate for the mechanical trouble through my skill. It worked for a few laps, but when I tried to pass another rider through the "woops" the bike's front suspension bottomed out hard and it felt like a giant had smacked my handle bars back. The violent motion resulted with my wrist being broken.

Obviously I didn't win that race. I was disappointed because my riding skill had grown to a level where I should have. Instead I didn't even finish.

My dad couldn't understand it either; he never seen me lose control that way. He became more concerned after he checked the bike and discovered that the suspension was totally out of tune. It looked like it had been purposely tampered with to make the bike impossible to control, let alone ride safely. In layman's terms, the right side of the suspension was much, much tighter than the left.

When we talked to the mechanic to see what he had to say he just shrugged his shoulders and shook his head. My dad and I could tell something was up, but it wasn't until two or three weeks later that we got the story. One of the mechanic's best friends was one of the riders I was racing against. The story that we got was that the mechanic had lost his fulltime job several weeks before the race and never told us. Just like the riders, the mechanics weren't making much money in the pits. The only thing that made any sense was that his buddy helped him out with a few bucks and in return he made sure that my bike would not be competitive.

Dad and I both wanted to be wrong, but it was the only conclusion that fit. So, we found a new mechanic and I let my wrist heal up for a few weeks.

Early on I was given a lot of advice on how to recover quicker: Different kinds of supplements or vitamins, rest, exercise, hot and cold treatments, the list is long. The one thing I have found that works for me is shark cartilage. I know that many of you think that I sound crazy, but I overdose on it every time I have had broken bone. I can't explain why, but I heal faster than anyone I know and I truly believe that the shark cartilage is a big reason why. You can call it one more of my secrets, if you like. And it is a secret that I would have to use a lot more in the years to come.

My right shoulder continued to give me problems. I could race, but it was agonizing and it affected my performance on the track. Later in the year I had it examined and told that I needed surgery to repair the damage from the crash and the doctor's screw-up. So I went under the knife for the first time. I was scared to death. Not because of the surgery, because of the down time. Even though I thought I was Superman, my body still needed time to recover and I wanted to get back on the track as soon as possible. I have noticed that doctors love to give advice and most of the time it is, "Rest." They didn't understand how committed I was to the sport. Within a week after my surgery I climbed on board my stationary exercise bike downing water and supplements and worked on maintaining my cardio fitness. It must have looked funny seeing a guy peddling with all of his might with his right arm in a sling. But it worked. When I started racing again I was finishing in top spots right away.

In 2001 I was competing at the World Mini National Championship in Las Vegas. I was at the top of my game and riding faster than ever. Midway through the race I was passed and on the next set of jumps I tried to get the first place position back. I hit the first lip too hard and as a result I entered the second jump with way too much momentum, wheel down. It caused the suspension to bottom out. My newly repaired right shoulder got seriously messed up again as it absorbed the shock of the landing, enough so that it had to be operated on again after less than a year. To add insult to injury, I also broke my collar bone in this crash. I remember when the paramedics wrapped me in bandages trying to hold the upper half of my torso together. It was a hundred and ten degrees and doing nothing to help my shoulder feel better. They ignored my pleas to unwrap me as I sweated heavily from the heat and pain.

At the beginning of 2003 I had a new Suzuki 125 and I took it for a test run on the Vegas track. The motorcycle had not been modified yet, but felt it was in good enough to try it out. My mistake. When you see those long, high jumps during motocross races you may think the rider does not have any control at that point. You would be wrong. I can use the torque of the bike to change its attitude in the air and adjust how it lands from the jump. Just a simple twist of the throttle. The problem this time was the bike was not properly tuned and in midair the engine died, leaving me helpless as the bike and I ended up landing upside down. I was shook up, but still was able to drive myself home. It wasn't until the next day at the doctor's office that I learned I had suffered my first concussion. I didn't have to wait long for my second one.

The next week my boot heel caught the lip of a jump on a practice run. It pulled me off the bike and bounced my body up so I ended up flying Superman style as I held onto the handle bars through the air. I didn't want to hit the dirt from thirty feet in the air without the benefit of the cushion of my bike's suspension, so in mid-air I was able to position my body so I could land on the bike. When I landed the springs bounced me off and I landed on my noggin again. I was getting tired of the headaches.

Later in 2003 I was racing in the Ponca City Amateur Nationals in Oklahoma. I went into one of the final races as the overall leader. I had not lost one single race. Then disaster struck. I guess my left shoulder was now jealous of the right, because the injury I sustained to it in the race required surgery to be repaired also. I was well into the lead when I came out of a turn. I was leaning over so far that my elbow dragged in the dirt hard enough to dislocate my left shoulder. I was getting tired of hearing that awful popping sound. It was midway through the year and plenty more races were on the schedule, so I talked my doctor into letting me finish out the season and postpone the surgery until early 2004. That gave me the opportunity to all but destroy my right ankle.

I was racing in the world mini-championships in Las Vegas late in the year doing well in the standings when in one of the turns my foot slipped off the peg of the bike and dug into the dirt at high speed. Strange feelings and sounds came from between the tips of my toes to right above my ankle. It reminded me of the snapping sounds carrots make when you break them in half. By the time I got back to the pits my foot looked like an eggplant. The doctor told me that I had torn a lot of the cartilage along with some damage to the tendons in my ankle.

By far my most frightening injury took place on a practice run in 2008. Every track is different, but this one felt plain goofy to me. The "woops" were carved out of the dirt in a way that made them almost impossible to handle. All the riders were choosing to go around them instead of jumping them. I was getting frustrated with the time the detour was adding to my laps, so I decided to attack to the "woops" and get the edge. Everything seemed to be going well until the last jump. On the landing I buried my front wheel and my body was thrown full force into the padded handle bars. Every bit of air that my lungs could hold was knocked out of me. I remember as a kid my mom telling me that you could die from having the air knocked out of you. I thought she was just trying to scare me into being careful. In fact it had happened to me before a couple of times and I was still alive to talk about it. But this time as my lungs screamed for air, I literally couldn't breathe and her words flooded my head.

I lay on the track begging my body to breathe as I started to become light headed. One of my friends was trying to help me and kept asking if I was okay. I couldn't catch my breath, let alone talk. Just when I thought it was going to be the end I was able to take a compulsive mini-breath. It was more of a hic-up and I could feel my body was starving for air, but the small amount of oxygen I was able to take in kept me from blacking out. It continued like that for a long time. It felt like I was drowning, but there was no water in sight. My breathing was gasping in little chirps. It would be days before I could take a deep breath. But on the track after a while I was able to get enough air in my lungs to where I could function and realize that this time I was really hurt. I had my friend take me to the emergency room.

Over the years I have grown accustomed to doctors looking at my x-rays and shaking their heads and then looking at me with disbelief. This time was no different. The doctor showed me the x-rays and explained that my sternum was cracked. The rib cage is a wonderful thing. It protects our internal organs from impacts like the one I had just endured. It is flexible and can take a hell of a shock, but this crash had pushed it to its limit. The part that sucked is that there was nothing they could do to help me. I had to endure that "rest" word again and was told that it would take some time to recover. I have to tell you, I am glad that I had the pad on my handle bars to absorb at least part of the impact. If I hadn't I might not be here today.

There have been several more injuries over the course of my career. My shoulders have been operated on six times and I suffered a back injury that could have messed me up for life. An inexperienced rider cut me off during a practice run and the result was having my bike land on top of me leaving a hematoma the size of a butt cheek on my back. But I'll spare you *all* of the details. I think you get the idea that motocross is a tough sport on the body. As a professional in this game, you cannot let the fear of getting hurt get to you. I do admit that in the first races after a major crash it's hard not to have that little tweak of fear in the back of your mind, but if I let that get to me it increases the chances that it will happen again. I have to maintain the focus on being the best and fastest and not on what might go wrong.

I wrestled with whether I should include all of my "big" injuries in this book. In the course of ten years I have had more emergency room visits and surgeries than most people have in several lifetimes. If you are looking to get started in the sport, you're probably scared to death. If you are a parent of an aspiring motocross racer you might be thinking about coaxing your kid into trying something safer, like sky diving or fire walking. The fans are wondering if it is worth it, but I still love it. All I can tell you is this: even though I have been hurt many times, I have loved every moment of my motocross career and at this point I can honestly tell you that every setback or injury I have endured pales in comparison to the joys of my accomplishments. I might be telling you a different story when I'm in my fifties and the aging process will be added to the old scars, but at this point I plan to go forward, continue with the risks and have the time of my life.

Wait until Obamacare gets a load of me!

CHAPTER 6
ATTITUDES

I learned early on that if I was going to become a successful motocross racer I would have to do it without any help from anyone outside my circle of family and friends. I wish could tell you that the sport is like one big happy family with people who help and encourage you in achieving your dreams, but that wouldn't be honest. For the most part it felt like me and my circle of friends against the world.

There were the exceptions like the families that camped out together in the pits when I was younger and the rare individual who would be willing to share his experiences with me, but for the most part the sport became more gritty as time went on. What was most frustrating was the attitude of the sponsors. After I crashed when the manager for Team Kawasaki was checking me out, my dad told me how hard it was even to get his attention. I remember meeting him and he had acted like he didn't want to be bothered by a kid who wanted to excel in the sport. I don't think he even remembered my name the day after the crash even though I was consistently finishing ahead of the racers on his team. As a top-sponsored racer and champion in the sport today, I bet he knows my name now; I still beat his riders.

I love people and care for everyone's happiness. When young riders come up to me at the races I make a point to be fully available to them and make sure that when they walk away they feel like they were treated with respect. My parents drilled the Golden Rule into my soul from day one; treat others the way you would like to be treated. It wasn't like that for me when I was coming up through the ranks.

There was a rider that I idolized when I was younger. He was always winning the major races and when I saw him on television interviews he seemed like the nicest guy in the world. I even had bought a pair of his old racing goggles. When you go to the tracks on race days, many of the racers have barrels or buckets filled with their used equipment for sale at cut rate prices. My dad bought me a pair of his goggles and I felt like I had hit the jackpot. I tried them on and imagined myself winning the races I had watched him win. I remember thinking that if I looked like him then I would have a better chance of being like him. A couple of months later we met at one of the national championships in California and he didn't give me the time of day, let alone talk to me about the sport. In fact he was a complete jerk. I gave the goggles away. What made things worse was that a mutual friend had told me that he overheard him say I didn't have what it takes to be a pro. That bothered me on a couple of levels. First it made me feel bad that I was busting my butt on the track and he was saying it wasn't enough. Second and more important I worried that as a heavily sponsored rider he might have influence with the sponsors I was trying to get.

Years later we got to know each other better as I moved up the ranks. We never became close friends, but we did have a healthy respect for each other. I once brought up his comments about me not having what it takes to be a pro. First he completely denied ever saying that. Then, after a few minutes, he apologized. "I knew you were good, but I didn't know you were that good!" he later told me.

That event and others like it have had a profound effect on how I try to treat others. I love the sport and when any fan wants to talk to me about my experiences, I am completely open. When a younger rider asks me for advice I make sure to be the best mentor I possibly can be. I remember what it felt like to be brushed off by so many of the different people I came across through the years and I made a vow to myself to never, ever, make anyone feel the way they made me feel. I also give most of my used equipment away to racers who need the financial help; I don't feel right selling it.

But, the negativity of the other people in the sport served as a motivation for me to try harder for the right reasons. The manager of the Kawasaki team made it easy for me to want to kick the butts of every one of his riders. And I did. Instead of getting frustrated with his actions I chose to take my energy and focus it on something useful. Winning.

Some of the most infuriating people around the tracks were some of the parents of other riders. The troublesome parents were in the minority when I first started out racing, but as my career continued the stakes got much higher and the riders who were not as serious about motocross began to disappear from the tracks and the concentration of wacked-out dads increased dramatically. I have countless memories of fathers screaming at their kids, some even hitting them, if they didn't win. Things like, "Do you know how much this is costing me?" and "That Costella kid is beating you, and his bike is crap!" echoed in the pits. Many of the dads felt that since they were spending a lot of money it bought them the right for their kid to win. Although it did give their riders an advantage in some ways, you can't buy talent at the shop. And talent is much more important, at least I think it is. But to win it takes heart, and there will never be a price tag on heart.

There were a few times when my dad and some of the other level-headed parents would have to get involved. More than a few times I saw parents taking swings at each other. The tension was immeasurable and there were a lot of reasons for it.

I added to the tension one day by raising the bar. I was still racing my KX-80 when I saw a seventy foot triple jump on a track I had never rode before. KX-80s were not supposed to be able to take on a jump of that magnitude and nowhere near that distance. Those types of jumps were put there for the big bikes with highly experienced riders. My rational brain said, "No way, don't even think about it!" But the lizard part of my brain won out: "Go for it!"

I told my dad I was going to jump it, and he looked at me like I had lost my mind. "You sure that's a good idea? It's a really big jump," he said with deep concern in his voice. He was right, most riders wouldn't even think about hitting a jump like that on bigger bike and here I was ready to try it on an 80?

I had the track to myself as I did a couple of fast laps to build up my courage. "Well, it's now or never!" I told myself. I shot out of the turn and set up for the jump. I knew I would make it the minute I hit the lip. It had been the farthest I had jumped a bike and I felt like I had conquered the world. I was actually laughing as the bike and I flew through the air. Right after I landed the jump I pulled off the track and everyone was in complete silence staring at me. It made me a nervous at first, but then I understood. They couldn't believe what they just saw. It was an awesome moment for me. Not so good for some of the other riders.

Many of the other dads started in on their kids right away. "He did it. With the bike I bought you it should be easy for you. Get out there and nail it!" None of the other riders even tried. It was way too scary. My dad just shook his head, "You know how to take chances, I'll give you that..." he said with a smile.

He was right; it was taking a big chance. Not only could I have messed up my body, I could have damaged my bike. That was another reason for all the pressure that the other dads were putting on their sons. Money. We were all still in the amateur class. Some of us had limited sponsors who gave us discounts on stuff, but the majority of the investment in our careers was out of our families' pockets. We had to watch every buck and even the cost of a replacement wheel made things harder. That was the way it was for me. My family had pretty much stretched out what money we had to keep me in the game. It was a balancing act. I had to take the risks to win and to get noticed by the sponsors, but I also had to do it without destroying my equipment.

It was also frustrating for me. Many of the other riders' parents had a lot more money than our family. It seemed like an unfair advantage at the time. For the most part, if other riders needed new bikes, their parents could afford it. If they wanted to modify the bikes, they had the resources to get it done. I was winning on a shoestring budget and a lot of the other dads took notice.

In 1999 I entered the California State Championships. I remember the looks the other racers and their families gave us as my dad and I were getting my bike ready. I loved my bike, but next to the other bikes it looked like it should have raced its last race ten races ago. All the other bikes were modified to the hilt. Mine was almost stock. When I heard the other riders and their dads make lame comments about my equipment it gave me the drive to finish first. Just like any sport, motocross is also an attitude sport. Think like a winner and your chances of winning go way up. Think like a loser, well you know. I was not going to let myself be beat by their bad attitudes.

The race went perfectly. I went out of the gate better than I ever had and nailed every turn and jump. An outsider to the sport would have thought that I had a supped-up bike, but I was what was supped-up and it paid off. Being named the state champion in front of all of the families who were making all the rude comments about me before the race was cool. Beating the riders of the Kawasaki team in front of the team manager was totally awesome. I didn't do it, but felt like walking up to him and asking, "Know my name now?"

I hated it when I heard the other dads yell at their kids and use me as ammunition for their rage. "The Costella kid is kicking your ass and his bike isn't half as good as yours." But I have to admit, knowing that I won the championship on a bike that was one of the least powerful on the track made it pretty easy for me to feel a rad.

Watching how many of the other dads acted toward their kids made me thankful for my dad. He never raised his voice to me. Not once. Every memory of my family at the beginning of my career was of love and encouragement. When I told them I wanted to try something new on the track, they helped me look for ways to make it work. If an emergency came up as far as money was concerned when we needed a new part, they would always try to figure out how to make it happen. There were many other kids on the track who had families that had a lot more money, but none of them had the love and support that I had that money can't buy. Not even close. But the financial strain did take its toll on my family.

In Felton, I never remember a raised voice in my house, except for my sisters and me getting into it over stupid stuff. My mom and dad always seemed like they were happy and everything was great and anyone who came to our house could feel the love our family generated. It was like that when we first moved to Vegas, too. But as the pressure increased with my motocross racing, so did the stress. Mom and dad had a lot to deal with. First of all they had the day-to-day things that every family deals with. Add that to having a son who is risking his life every weekend and having to come up with the money so he could do it, well let's just say that it was a recipe for extreme stress. It didn't happen often, but mom and dad would argue about how to manage my career and how to find the money so I could continue. I hated it but understood it at the same time, even though I was still pretty young, being in my late teens. I also recognized the pressure it was putting on the other motocross families. I remember constantly praying for a sponsor to notice me and sign me up so I could take the financial pressure off my parents. At the same time I thanked the Lord for having a family which loved me enough to believe in and help me achieve my dreams.

A few months after the disaster of the crash when the Kawasaki guy was checking me out, my dad sat me down and let me know where things stood. I could see how hard it was on him to have to tell me that my racing had gotten to a point where it might not be possible for my parents to afford for it to continue. Even though we had a new local sponsor that helped us with the cost of the bikes and the parts, it wasn't enough. I wanted to race every race I could. My thinking was the more I was out there beating the sponsored riders, the better my chances of getting picked up by a big time sponsor. The problem was that the races were all over the nation and the travel costs alone were too restrictive for me to compete in all of them.

I felt like grabbing a soap box, setting it up in the middle of a track in an arena full of fans, jumping on it and screaming, "LOOK AT ME! I'M BEATING ALL OF THE SPOSORED RIDERS AND THEY WON'T EVEN TALK TO ME!!!" It was a nice thought, but not very practical. Instead my dad and I decided we would compete in the local races, some in California, with the best equipment we could afford. On my own I decided that I would become the racer that was impossible to ignore every time I had a chance to race in front of a crowd.

Before my dad explained the money part of my racing, I would feel a little sorry for myself knowing that most of the riders I was racing against had better equipment. I also envied the riders who had the money to travel as far as the East Coast to compete. But then I decided to change my thinking and, instead of dwelling on what I didn't have, I would focus on what I did have and make the absolute best I could out of it. I was used to beating riders who were riding better bikes than me and seeing ones that I was beating being picked up by some of the bigger sponsors. I figured I had made it this far on limited resources, I might as well do whatever I had to do to accomplish my goal to become a professional motocross racer. In short, I developed an unbeatable attitude, but it also took some lucky breaks to keep me on the track along the way.

I picked up a new local sponsor, Carter Power Sports. They believed in my ability and went the extra mile to help me stay competitive. When the bike I was racing got to the point where it was no longer able to reasonably keep up on the track, they would sell it and apply every bit of the profit to a new bike at a deeply discounted price. It kept me on the track. I got support from my doctor. When my shoulder was blown out the first time my family had to make monthly payments for my treatment. On more than one occasion the doctor told my dad that he could skip a month's payment and that would be enough to cover the tires and fuel I needed to race. I had so many little blessings, which were really big blessings, that I was able to keep on racing without bankrupting my family.

It didn't take away the pressure. Lining up on the gates knowing that the bike I was on was the least likely to win and the only way to have a chance was to outride all the other riders amped-up my mental intensity. I had to be the most aggressive rider to have a chance at winning, so I made sure that I was the most aggressive rider. In the year after my first big crash I never finished outside of the top five spots. Most of the time I was in the top three, and many, many times I won. Knowing I did this on a bike that was not as good as the others on the track took my confidence level to new heights and made me even harder to beat. I believe this is when I defied the odds and the scientists and learned how to use my will, heart, and determination to get more out of the bike than should have been physically possible. I know it sounds crazy, but if another rider can get ten more horsepower out of a bike, I can get eleven.

It was a long year, but it was a good year considering what I had to do to stay competitive on the track. At the end of 1998 I was getting ready for one of the bigger races in Las Vegas. My dad and I had tuned and tweaked every last bit of horsepower and torque out of my tired bike and felt that I had a good shot at taking the first place trophy. Overall the bike was okay, but I was a little nervous that it might not be able to handle what I would have to put it through to win the race, but it was the only bike I had and it would have to do.

A few nights before the big race I was getting ready: I cleaned and polished my Suzuki RM 125 to the point that a novice would think it was brand new. It would take someone with a lot of experience in the sport to see that the bike was on its last legs. Then I went inside and ironed my name and number, "129," on my jersey and hit the sack. The next day everyone at school was wishing me luck with the upcoming race. I was getting excited thinking that maybe this would be the race where a sponsor would notice me and take the financial load off my family.

I had a ritual when I got home after school. I would go straight to the fridge and grab something to drink then go out to the garage and fool around with my bike. It had been a habit for years. This time after I grabbed the water and walked out the door that connected the kitchen to the garage I knew something was wrong. Before the door opened all the way I noticed that there was daylight in the garage and the alarms in my head were blaring as I threw the door open. My motorcycle was gone.

It's funny how things run through your mind when you are faced with a violation or disaster. First I thought that dad had taken the bike to get a once over at the shop before the big race, then I tried to convince myself that I left my bike in the backyard.

I never had done that before, but I wanted to believe anything besides the truth. It was stolen.

It felt like a crook had reached into my chest and ripped out my heart. The garage was open when I got home, but I was so used to my routine that I didn't notice. Mom might have just left for the store and forgot to push the button to close the door, maybe Nina came in the house though there, whatever, I didn't even think about checking for my dirt bike. Now as I looked at the bare spot on the floor where my bike was supposed to be, my stomach churned. It was gone and, with it, any chance to be in the big race next weekend. I felt like I was crushed by a wrecking ball and dragged to the dump.

My parents got home not long after my discovery and they took it just as hard as I did. It was more than a theft of the motorcycle; it was like someone had dissected our dream.

The race was only days away and we didn't have the money to replace the bike. Even if we could get insurance to cover it, it would be too late to make it to the race that was so important. For the first time in my life I felt truly beaten. Then my family, again, stepped up to the challenge and went to bat for me.

My sister contacted a local news station right away and convinced them that the heartbreak of a stolen motorcycle from an upcoming motocross racer would make a great public interest story. Maybe it was just to get her to shut up and stop calling or a slow news day, but the reporter showed up on our doorstep with his camera crew within a few hours. I think the impact of how close my family was and how important it was for them to help me impressed the reporter; he took the story very seriously.

Later that night we sat around the TV watching the local news when the segment about my stolen bike went on the air. It was weird seeing all of us on the small screen and a little embarrassing at the same time. Kids had stuff stolen from them all of time, why was my loss so important?

The reporter did a great job explaining about my aspirations and how this was much more than a story about a stolen dirt bike, it was about a life-changing event in a young man's life. Although I was touched with the efforts of my sister, I went to bed that night feeling completely deflated. There was no way I was going to able to be in the races next weekend and it would be a long time before we had the money to get another bike to race. The dream was in big trouble.

I was also feeling a little guilty. A couple of weeks before, Nina had scratched the family car while backing it out of the garage. She begged me not to tell our parents and I finally agreed. When my mom and dad got home they were livid and demanded to know what happened. I tried to keep my word, but when dad told he was going to take my dirt bike away if I didn't tell him right then and there what happened, I freaked out. I turned around and pointed at Nina and screamed, "She did it!" Now she was getting the local news involved to try and help get my bike back.

I was so depressed that I didn't want to go to school the next day, but my mom made me. The thought of having to see all of my friends was discouraging, especially after my disaster was on television the night before. I didn't want to talk about it. I wanted to crawl under a rock and be left alone. Thankfully mom was right. I had a ton of people come up to me and share their concerns about what had happened. At lunch a friend came up to me with some unexpected news.

"Derek, I know who took your bike!" My heart felt like it stopped. "I think I can get it back for you, but you have to keep the cops out of it. This guy is a bad dude. He has guns and knives." It was a lot to digest for a sixteen year old, but I just wanted my bike back. The race was a couple of days away and I needed to be in it.

"Okay, no cops! I just want my bike. I don't care about anything else, just do whatever it takes to get it back!" I looked him in the eye, "Please."

He said, "Okay, I'll try. If it works out I'll bring it to your house after school."

The rest of the day was the longest afternoon of my life. Would I get my bike back? I wanted to believe I would, but at the same time I was afraid to get my hopes up after stewing all night about being bike-less. After school I went straight home, only this time I didn't go in and get a drink. I put my books down and sat on the curb and prayed. Then I heard it. A dirt bike was coming up the street and before I could see it I started to feel the pangs of hope that it was my bike. And it was. My friend pulled onto my driveway and handed the motorcycle to me. "You have to keep this quiet, okay?"

"Don't worry about it, I won't say a word to anyone. I'm just happy to get it back, thanks!" I said.

As he walked out of the neighborhood I couldn't help but wonder if he was the one who stole my dirt bike or if he really did stick his neck out and help me get it back from a bad guy. It didn't matter, I was back in the race that was only a day away.

The looks on my family's faces when they got home and saw the bike back in the garage will be an image that I will cherish forever. We could not believe how blessed we were and I couldn't thank my sister enough for going to the news station and pushing them to do the story. I felt like I had just won the biggest race yet. But, I had a race to get ready for and no time to lose, so my dad and I started in on the bike. We went through it as carefully as we could and everything seemed to be good. It ran well and I was confident that I could take it on the track and win.

When I went to bed that night I looked up at the ceiling and thought about the events of the last year or so. I thought about sponsors, the other racers and their families and how I was competing on bikes that were not up-to-speed compared to the other bikes on the tracks. And I was still here. I had a very real fear that I would be out of motocross racing for a while when my dirt bike was stolen. But, I was going to race the next day because I got lucky, but I prefer to say blessed.

I started to understand that I had learned how to make the most out of what I had, which was a lot, and get more out of it than should have been possible. My parents said it was because I had a good attitude and was always willing to give it my all. Part of me agreed but I also felt like I was still in the sport because I was meant to be in it. I fell asleep the night before the race knowing that it didn't matter what happened, good or bad, I was going to be a pro some day.

My mind was buzzing with the events of the last year when I pushed my bike up to the gates for the start of the race. I had won a national championship despite the odds. I dislocated my shoulder in a bad crash. I also saw how the financial pressures my racing had put a lot of stress on my family. All in all it had been a crazy year for both good and bad reasons. I tried to push the thoughts out of my mind and focus on what I had to do now. Win the race, no matter what.

I got a great start and at the end of the first lap I had a lead that would be hard to beat. Then my engine blew up. Later, dad and I figured that when the bike was stolen the crooks had probably pushed the engine way too hard, red lining the tachometer too many times. There was no way we could have known that the bike was toast before the race even started.

It was a sickening sound as metal ground against metal as the pistons gouged into the cylinder walls of my engine and I knew right away that my race was over. I pushed my bike off the track and rested it on its side, pulled off my helmet and sat on it. I put my head into my hands and tried to figure out just how I was going to make it to the pros. This was a setback, but I would not let it be the end. I was more resolved than ever that I would accomplish the goal, I just didn't know how.

CHAPTER 7
NO REGRETS

I remember listening to an interview of Andre Agassi a while ago, the one time world tennis champion who inspired millions and was also a resident of Las Vegas. I have a lot of respect for him because his charities have helped a ton of people. He also started his career very young, like me. He talked about what it was like growing up. When he talked about his childhood I am sure that most listeners felt sorry for him. He talked about the fact that he didn't have the average childhood, if any at all. He went into detail about marathon practice sessions on the tennis court, extensive travel, intensive physical training and having little or no time for the stuff that average teenagers do. He also talked about how he sometimes felt a sorry for himself wishing that he could live a life more like his friends. When I listened to his interview I felt the same compassion that I am sure the other listeners felt, but I also clearly understood what it was like for him. Like him, my entire life revolved around the sport I pursued, his was tennis and mine was motocross. Unlike him, I never felt like I was making any kind of sacrifice to excel in motocross, it was all I wanted to do.

I cannot tell you why or where it came from, but as far back I can remember I have always been obsessed with doing whatever it took to have a shot at being a pro in my sport. I told you before that my biggest fear was "not finishing," but to be honest it goes deeper than that. I never wanted to be in a position where I would have to tell myself, "I wish had I tried harder." It has affected every aspect of my life. I think it makes me a better son, brother, friend and husband today. It definitely made me more aggressive and hard to beat on the track. But when I was young I was willing to commit myself to do whatever it took to get better at anything I wanted to be good at and follow through with all of the actions it took to make it happen. In short, I made it a point to live my life with no regrets.

I think there were laws that prevented me from working before I was fifteen and a half, but as soon as I hit that milestone I hit the pavement to find work. I knew that the financial pressures were building for my parents and I wanted to help and working with my dad was no longer an option. He began working for another company and having his son tag along with him wouldn't work. I quickly found out that job opportunities for kids that were fifteen were extremely limited, but I persisted. I finally lucked out and got hired as a bag boy at a major grocery store. It wasn't the most glamorous job in the world, but I was thankful for the opportunity. And the paycheck.

I was already fully engulfed in my pursuit of getting sponsored, but as soon as I got my first job my schedule got even more intense. I would get up early to make sure that my bike and equipment were ready for that night's practice laps or races. Then I would give it my all at school. My education was always super important to me, I didn't want to be an adult who had trouble reading or not knowing how to balance a checkbook. After school I would go straight to work.

I took it seriously, but I have to admit I did have a little fun while I was on the clock. How could a dare devil motocross racer resist the pull of shopping carts! My co-workers and I would take the powered ones for the handicapped and have races with them, not as thrilling as attacking the track on my motorcycle, but a great diversion. We had different events and the best time was always the target. We would make it fun by mixing it up. Who could get the best time riding the carts backwards was just one of the variations. If I could have figured out a way to jump them I would have, but they were pretty slow and way too heavy. When it came time to pick up the regular shopping carts out of the parking lots and bring them back into the store, we often were racing to see who could get the most back inside the fastest. Once in a while I would sneak out to my truck and listen to one of my favorite songs, one of my few breaks in the day. (Sorry, Vons.)

After work I was off to the gym. I used the money I was earning, which wasn't very much, to hire a personal trainer. It was expensive, so I didn't have as many sessions as I wanted, but I was able to take what I learned and become much more effective when I was working out on my own. It felt funny always being the youngest guy in the gym, but I was focused on getting into the best shape that I could.

After the workout I was off to the track more often than not. My morning diligence to my equipment gave me more time on the track to hone my skills. I made a point to practice every aspect of racing. Jumps, turns and finding the ways to maintain control of the bike under any circumstances were my priorities and my riding was improving weekly. I never had a problem sleeping because every night when I got home I was completely exhausted, in a good way. That was pretty much my daily routine Monday through Thursday. Get up, take care of the bike, bust butt in school, go to work, go to the gym, practice on the track, come home and crash hard. Friday through Sunday is when things got mixed up.

Sometimes my dad and I would be in our garage getting ready for the local races that were being held in Vegas on Friday nights. Other times we were loading up the bikes and getting ready for the late night drive to the out-of-town races to California, Utah and many of the other tracks where I needed to be to pursue my dreams. The weekends were all about racing the bike or practicing on the track. We would get home late Sunday night. Monday morning started the repeat of the week before.

Sometimes I would be able to hang around with my friends for short periods of time, but for the most part my schedule was pretty unforgiving. I made a point to have meals with my best friend, Chad, once in awhile. We both shared the geeky obsession with motorcycles. Other than that most of my free time and money, what little there was of it, was devoted to motocross.

I was spending most of the money I was making from my part time job on the sport I loved so much. Here is another one of those little secrets I told you about. When there was time, Chad and I would throw an old fuel drum on the back of the truck and head up to the Boulder City. It was about thirty miles away from my house and had a small airport catering to general aviation. At the time it would cost about a buck a gallon to fill the tank in your car. Racing fuel was costing well over five. Aviation fuel was selling for about two and a half dollars and was better for racing. It was leaded and easier on the engine of my motorcycles because the lead would lubricate the internal parts. I would mix the aviation fuel with the racing fuel and I still think it gave me a little bit of an edge over the competition in the races.

I did spend a little of my earnings on things other than motocross. My dad loved aquariums. As long as I could remember he had a fascination with them, so I put aside some money from my first pay checks and surprised him and my mom one day with a new fish tank. They were stoked and I was happy to give them something that they enjoyed so much.

So, at a fairly young age I learned a work ethic that would intimidate most. From the moment I woke in the morning until the time I hit the sack most of my time was completely filled. I never felt sorry for myself even though I was tired many times. I remember a couple of times when customers would ask me questions at the store. I would hear the sound come out of their mouth, but didn't really understand what they were saying because of my zombie state of mind. I would just look at them blankly and say, "Huh?"

The extra money that I brought in helped a lot in the pursuit of my dreams, but I knew something else was going to have to happen fast if I was going to make it as a pro. As my career progressed, so did the cost. It was becoming a money monster with an endless appetite and it was getting harder and harder to feed. By starting to work and bringing in a little extra money the monster wasn't eating us up completely yet, but my dad and I knew it was always right there behind my rear fender ready to take a big bite out of the checking account.

CHAPTER 8
OUT OF THE BLUE

I have told you about some of the negative parts of my career. The injuries, setbacks and having to deal with the mega-sized egos of some of the people of the sport. I have also have had to witness some pretty scary stuff.

I remember having to watch a poor kid get totally abused by his father. We were at the Golden State Championships in 2000 and the rider had broken his leg in a race three weeks before. In a qualifying race he had a bad crash on one of the turns and re-fractured his leg. His dad was screaming at him to get up and finish and also told him that if he didn't compete in the championship he would have to walk home. Everyone could see that the rider was seriously hurt, but his dad didn't seem to care. He wanted his rider back on the track no matter what. The pressures in the sport can be that intense and cause people to act completely unreasonable. After seeing that, it made me thankful for my family which motivated me through support, not intimidation.

As I look back, I recall hundreds of moments that warm my heart and bring me a smile, also. Some of the moments were fairly small and of little consequence. Maybe a competitor would offer to lend me a part I needed to compete or I would win a race when I thought I didn't have a chance. Others turned out to be pretty important in the big picture of my career. There was one, however, that changed things for me for the good and may be the single-most important reason, outside of my immediate family or my control, why I was able to accomplish what I have in motocross. Some might call it blind luck, others may say it was the fluke of flukes. All I know is that it showed me that I was meant to make it in motocross, although it is not what I could have ever expected.

Part of me wished that it had happened sooner, but now I am actually glad it didn't. Having to struggle at the start of my journey wasn't fun. It would have been easier, I guess, if we had a ton of money or had the sponsors signed me on right away. It might have been nice if from the start I had had access to everything I needed to be truly competitive and not have to stress about how I was going to get it. I now understand that not having those options made me a much better rider. Yes, I had to pay a higher price, not the least being racing on equipment that was not as good as most of the other riders. Having to do that makes me appreciate my success all the more. But, nevertheless, God smiled on me in 2001.

***

A couple of weeks after my engine blew up in the first lap of the Vegas race my family was trying to figure out how we were going to get another bike so I could get back on the track. I knew my dad was at the end of his rope, both emotionally and financially. I remember watching him pace and chain smoke cigarettes trying to blow off some of the stress on race days. I also knew that if I had better equipment I would be able to get the attention of the sponsors faster and take the load off my family. It was a true catch 22 situation — we needed more money so we could take off the pressures when it came to money.

Then I got my first big sponsor in a very unconventional manner, but a blessing nevertheless. We got the phone call one night and were told that one of my sister's sisters-in-law and her family had made some savvy investments and they paid off. Big time. Nothing short of a life changer as far as money was concerned. Living in Vegas I hear about people running into big money all the time, but having a family member come into big bucks in a more conventional manner is mind boggling, especially on Las Vegas standards.

Not long after their investments paid off, they called up my mom and dad and invited them to a nice dinner in a fancy restaurant and made my parents a proposal. They had been watching me over the years and knew how serious I was about my career in motocross and wanted to help me out by sponsoring me. Not only did they want to help out, they agreed to invest whatever it took to help me become a sponsored champion. Like I said, I have an awesome family.

They had a lot of requests from a bunch of other people both inside and outside the family and they helped many, but they looked at me to make an investment into my future. It wasn't like I decided to go into motocross after they came into the big money, my family had seen my commitment to the sport from the very beginning. Some kids grow up wanting to become doctors or lawyers. All I ever wanted to do was to become a fully sponsored professional motocross racer, so instead of needing financial help for law or medical school, I needed help with the equipment. You can say their help was more of a scholarship. It wasn't an open checkbook. We all agreed that they would help me get sponsored, which had always been the dream, and there were limits on both time and how much they were willing to invest. But, it was fun for them to be able to help get a kid on his way to become a professional athlete. My parents were still investing a lot of money, but the help was very much appreciated and needed.

It was such huge blessing for us on so many levels. Right away we could feel the pressure lift off and the infrequent bickering in the house between mom and dad ended. Because of that, we were also able to enjoy the journey more. Before, there was so much pressure knowing that if I didn't get sponsored soon that I might have to put my career and more importantly, my dream, on hold because of money. It was like having a Honda Goldwing hanging by a thread over our heads; it could have dropped and crushed the dream at any moment. It also felt great knowing that I was going to be able to get the best equipment under my butt and not have to worry about travel expenses, entry fees and all the other expenses that come with the sport. I also could compete in all of the important races and classes, no matter where they were in the country. It made me a better racer because I knew that the new situation would remove any possible excuses. Before the big money hit, I could say that the other riders were on better equipment. Now, if I got beat, it was because of me and only me. Believe me, I was more than ready for the challenge.

Once my parents ironed out the details with my relatives I felt like I got twenty Christmases in one day. Before, when we went to the shops and looked for bikes and equipment we always had to keep the cost in mind. Now the only consideration was speed and performance. I was in Motocross heaven. But, first we had to do some research.

We knew that my extended family's sponsorship was temporary and the ultimate goal was to get a more traditional big-time sponsor, fast. But, which one? I had a pretty bad taste in my mouth after my experience with the manger of the Kawasaki team, so I didn't even consider them. I just wanted to beat their riders every chance I got. I thought their bikes were great: how they treated people wasn't. After talking to many of the motocross gurus we found out that the ultimate ride, as far as sponsors were concerned, was Suzuki. They took motocross and its riders more seriously than other sponsors. They provided the most and best equipment and had the highest earnings potential. So, after a lot of prayers, my family and I decided that Suzuki was the target. Then we went shopping.

I have a friend who has an unconventional method for picking out his younger children's birthday presents. He got tired of his kids playing with the boxes an hour after they opened the toy, so instead of going shopping ahead of time and hoping that he picked out the gifts that his kids wanted, he takes them with him. He tells the birthday boy or birthday girl they can get anything they want and how much they can spend. Then he takes them to the toy store. He seats them in the shopping cart and pushes them up and down the aisles filled with toys and the excited kid points and says, "I want that and that and that!" He takes the items off the shelves and puts them in the cart and says, "Okay, what else do you want?" What makes it funny is that he doesn't let anyone know that it is his kid's birthday. On more than one occasion he has heard other children in the store yelling at their moms, "Why does that kid get everything he wants, that's not fair!"

I have an idea of what it felt like for his kids. Once we figured out how we should attack my career, what we needed to make it happen and had a real budget to work with, we walked into the motorcycle shop with my shopping list. I started to point and fill the cart, so to speak. "I need two new dirt bikes so I can compete in multiple classes, these wheels that are lighter and more durable, those shocks that are a better fit for my weight and that engine-modifying kit to get the most horsepower out of the new motorcycle to race in the unlimited class." Seeing the other customers' expressions in the shop made me feel spoiled. But, it also felt really, really good. I remembered when I was a little envious of some of the other riders at the tracks who had parents that had the money to race with the stuff I was getting now.

It was a long list. We got two Suzuki RM 125s and an RM 250. Then came the stuff to modify them to be race-ready: after-market clutches, grips, fenders, wheels, hubs, spokes, sprockets, seat covers, frame guards, handlebars, I could go on and on and on. Then we needed something to haul all the new stuff around the country as we went from race to race, so we got a new trailer complete with workbench, generator, tools, and equipment to secure the bikes while we were on the road. We had graphics put on the trailer with the goal of having more and more sponsors' names being added quickly. The biggest logo was "Herrero Racing" in honor of my family members who were footing the bill. I still smile when I remember other riders coming up to me at the pits asking, "'Herrero Racing,' who are they?"

I just smiled and said, "The best sponsors in the world!"

Then we had a lot of the day-to-day expenses. The motor work alone could add up to five hundred bucks a month. We also had the hotel expenses, travel cost, entry fees, and the yearly association fees. All-in-all it added up to a lot of money and, although I did have a few sponsors before, I was starting to get a taste of what it was like for the big time riders. And I liked it.

It was truly motivating for me. I had dreamed for so long what it would feel like to be able to race with top-notch equipment. I was still having a lot of fun and as long as I was on the track I was happy. However being able to select exactly what I needed to be the most competitive was addicting and I made a point to never again be in the position where I had to worry about the bike I was on. *I was going to get sponsored soon* and I didn't care what I would have to do to make it happen. Plus, I didn't have any more excuses.

Looking back, I still honestly believe that I would have made it in the sport even without the additional financial support, but I also know it would have taken much longer and may have even been more dangerous. Pushing equipment past its prime has risks all its own. I never took the blessing for granted and never forgot all of the sacrifices my family made on my behalf before the big money hit. But I also know that the blessing wasn't just for me, it was for all of us for so many different reasons. To this day I am deeply thankful for everyone's support.

I told you before about my trainer who explained to me that a motocross race was like a war. I had been a warrior from the very beginning of my racing. Now I had the shiny new armor and all of the ammunition I needed to be the most competitive. I remember thinking to myself, "Wait till they get a load of me now…"

CHAPTER 9
JEKYLL AND HYDE

Many of the people who know me think I am schizophrenic, and they might be right. I am two different people. Off the track I am most likely one the goofiest guys you would ever meet. I like to joke around and make people laugh. I have been known to push the envelope too far as to what is socially acceptable. If I am surrounded by people who are happy and in a good mood, I am comfortable. If I'm not, I do whatever it takes to bring the mood up. It takes a whole lot fewer muscles to smile than to frown, so in my heart I feel we should always be looking for reasons to have fun and feel good. Sometimes I drive my friends nuts when they are trying to be serious about something that really isn't all that important. I'll toss out off-the-wall jokes or do something crazy to bring them back into my world. It is just part of who I am. I walk out of movies that make me sad and I hate it when people are unhappy so I am willing to do whatever it takes to make them feel better. Then there is my other side. When the gates go down and the race starts, it is like I took a shot of intensity juice and I cannot care less what anyone is thinking or feeling, except for me. And I only feel like winning.

To say that I am competitive would be too simple. It might be a plain old fashion desire to win or some twisted gene that kicks in, but I become a completely different person when the race starts. To be honest, sometimes it scares me. There is a scene in the Kevin Costner movie, "For the Love of the Game," when he walks up to the pitcher's mound in a big league baseball game with a huge mass of fans roaring all around him. He tells himself to tune them out and all the noise and the distractions stop. He is alone on the mound. I know exactly what that feels like, but I don't have to tell myself to tune out the distractions, it happens automatically.

I have overheard many people in the pits on many different occasions say that I was this super fast, crazy, out-of-control racer. They were partly right, I was and am super fast, but I am always in control. And I might be a little crazy; I think I have to be to win. It may look like I'm out of control when I am on the track, but I know how to push me and my bike past our limits. An outsider's point of view might see a crazy kid holding on to his bike for dear life; it might even look a little spastic. But those who know the sport see that I am just pushing the envelope very, very hard. There are no such things as comfort zones in a race. If you are comfortable, you are going to lose. You have to be willing to go well beyond comfortable and be willing to take the risks that may seem crazy but are needed if you are going to have a shot at placing in the top spots. The real trick is finding the balance that lies somewhere between what you *know* you can do in each lap to get the fastest speed and what you *have* to do to earn the victory. One of my big advantages is that I almost never crash no matter how hard I push in each lap. You have to be willing to push yourself well beyond your limits, even if you are not exactly sure what your limits are. You can't win by crashing, and you can't win by holding back even just a little bit. Thank God for adrenaline. It helps me find and stay on that razor sharp edge that I must have to win.

I have also been blessed with strong self-discipline, so I can do what I have to do off the track to stay in winning shape. But

I always make it fun and people on the outside might even think I'm dorky. My mom always calls me Perk, short for Perky. It would be safe to say that I like to joke around a lot, all the time. But when it comes to a race, the only thing that exists in my universe is the bike, me, and the track. And it feels like we are one. When I hit the first turn of a race, I'm not a husband, friend, son, or brother. I'm not even sure if I am part of the human race; my focus and intensity are that powerful and the adrenalin pumping through my body fine-tunes them to the sharpest of edges. I believe having to race on equipment that wasn't the fastest on the track or the most reliable strengthened this quality. So when my relatives sponsored me I had the best of both worlds. Now I raced on the best bikes with the mental focus I had learned before that blessing. At the risk of sounding a little cocky, I almost felt invincible. But there was also a new pressure.

Before, the thought of being picked up by a big time sponsor was more of a dream. I took it very seriously, but in the back of my mind I knew it was going to be hard with the inferior bikes I was racing on. Now, being able to race on the fastest bikes out there, the dream became a more achievable goal and the clock was ticking. Suddenly when the gates dropped, I didn't just race to win the checkered flag, I also raced to earn the career I wanted. Knowing that I had a very real shot of making the dream come true made each race all the more important. And the year and a half after I started to ride the best bikes with the best equipment became the longest race of my life.

Not only did I have the best equipment, I had more of it. Having more bikes allowed me to compete in more classes and races. I also had the resources to compete in many more events across the country. It was simple mathematics, the more I raced the more my name was announced over the loud speakers. The more I won, the more pictures were taken of me and I received more recognition. It all added up to more, more, more. My name was getting out there and my reputation of being a great rider was getting bigger and better by the day. Looking back, it seems like a whirlwind, but at the time it was exhausting, in a good way.

I began to compete in countless races across the country, so much so that I had to pull out of classes and earn my diploma through home schooling. Road schooling may be a more accurate description since I was doing a lot of my schoolwork between races far from home. I had always wanted to be a pro racer, but getting my diploma was just as important to me. As it should be for you.

There are a few races that stick out in my mind in the year and a half that I was going after the team Suzuki sponsorship full-on, and I believe to this day that they were the most important. All the races counted, but these proved to be milestones in my career.

The first was the Golden State Nationals in 2000. It was one of the biggest races in the country and held in Southern California. I had competed in it before, but now I believed I could win with my new equipment. I was also racing in a higher class, so the other riders I was racing against were the best I had ever gone up against. Without naming names, there were many nationally known riders, most of which were sponsored big-time and I felt like I was in heaven to be on the same track with them. I wasn't considered a newcomer because I had been around the tracks for a while, but this was the first time that many thought I could be a real threat to win the championship. There was one racer that sticks out in my mind who tried to stand in my way of becoming a company-sponsored rider. I shouldn't mention his name. Okay, his name was Dillon Lord. He had been a sponsored Suzuki rider for couple of years.

We both qualified to race in the championship and everyone there knew that it would probably be one of us who would win. I had always been taken seriously on the track, but I think

I intimidated the other riders when I showed up with top-notch equipment. I remember overhearing one of them saying, "Uh oh" under his breath as I pulled my new, fully modified bike up to the gates.

It still amazes me that a time span of only twenty minutes or so can have such a huge impact on my life, but it did and still does. Everything rides on the time between the moment the gate drops and the winner passes the finish line. I went into this race completely aware of just how important it was for me to win. There were a few Team Suzuki riders racing against me. My thinking was that if I wanted to get sponsored by Suzuki, beating their best riders on their best equipment couldn't hurt my chances at all.

The track was one of the most brutal in the country and that, along with my crazy style, gave the fans a most entertaining race to watch. The intensity of this race amped it up even more. I got a great start and hit the first turn with the lead and quickly built it to a four bike-length cushion. Even though I had a good lead I was still nervous; I wanted to win this race for so many different reasons. I could also feel Lord catching up. It wasn't like he was ready to overtake me, but I could feel him reeling me in and it rose my adrenaline level all the more. The track had a brutal double S-turn carved out of the mountain. Taking it the at a high speed on your own in a practice lap was enough to unnerve you a little, having to navigate it in a championship race was another thing altogether.

As we entered the first part of the turn I could feel Lord right on my back fender. I had lost the cushion of a bike length's lead but was still confident that I could stay in front. I had a plan in my mind on how to build my lead back up as we were halfway through the first part of the first S-turn when my bike washed out. I am certain I had a little help from Dillon tapping my back tire with his front, thus causing the crash. I was as angry as I had ever been as he flew past me.

My bike's engine was still running and in a millisecond I was back on my ride determined to do whatever it took to get the lead back. I have told you before that I believe a rider's intensity level can squeak out more power from the engine and make the tires hold on to the track better. It defies all science, but I know firsthand that it is true and it was this race that proved it to me. I was getting great lap times before the washout, but now I cut several seconds off each lap and the only difference was me. The track was the same, the bike was also, but I was pissed and every bit of energy and focus the emotion caused somehow transferred into my equipment and made me faster. The energy literally cut four or five seconds off my lap times, which is a big deal. I didn't care if I crashed and the only thought going through my head was that I was going to win this race no matter what. Nothing else mattered. And I was also going to beat Lord at his own game.

I quickly caught up to Lord and we went into the same turn that I went down in a couple of laps earlier. This time there was a completely different result. He thought I was going to grab the lead back by taking the outside line. It would have made sense because that is what I normally would have done, but this time I dropped my bike into the inside line then let it drift up on the burm forcing the other rider way too high on the lip of the turn. Instead of slowing down and letting me pass, he tried to beat me out of the turn by adding throttle. Instead of shooting out and into the next part of the S-turn, he flew off the top of the turn as I retook the lead.

A few seconds later I was in the middle of the next jump and turned my head to see where Lord was. I was almost in shock as I saw what had unfolded. He and his bike flew off the track and ended up in a spectator area. Instead of stopping, he gunned it, got back on the track and came after me. I guess I'm not the only one who can use his anger to increase his desire to win. I had about a five-second lead as we went through a long straight-a-way that led into a huge turn. I could feel him catching up as I entered the turn, then I let my bike ride to the top of the turn and slowed a little so he could catch up. It was time to give him a second dose of his own medicine. When he passed me I opened the throttle all the way on my bike and by the time we entered the next turn I pulled the same trick as before and sent him flying off the track again. It must have been like watching two pit bulls fighting to the crowd. Neither of us was going to back down and we wanted to taunt each other into making mistakes.

This time my aggressive riding paid off. I had the lead back and kept it all the way to the finish line. As I look back I have to admit that instead of being mad at Dillon Lord for washing me out at the beginning of our battle in the race, I am thankful he did it. He might have provided me with that extra edge I needed to win. There are a ton of great riders out there and he was one of the best. If he hadn't had pissed me off so much maybe I would have come in second place instead. But the fireworks weren't over yet.

I wasn't proud of myself for being so aggressive on the track, but I was still so mad that I could spit. Then came a big surprise. I half expected to be harassed in the pits, but instead a lot of other riders and their families come up to me thanking me, say-ing what a great job I did and that Lord had it coming. I found out that he had a reputation of being a punk both on and off the track and he was not the most popular rider out there. Then I had to face him and his family. I was still worked up and was longing for a fight. Even though I out-rode him and beat him at his own game, I was still swimming in the anger his actions brought out in me during the first part of the race when he made me washout on the turn. I didn't like the way I was feeling.

I am not an aggressive person off the track. I hate violence and deeply believe that motocross should be a sport of skill and not aggression. When I race, I do it to win, but I also want to win cleanly, not by taking other riders out. But, if you want to come after me that way, then I am going to come after you that way, only ten times harder and I promise you that it's not going to be pretty. It's more than just payback, it's an altered state I go into that is fueled not only by the desire to win, but also the desire to see the sport played out the way I think it should be. I want to see the best rider win, even if it is not me that day. Not the guy who wins by making others crash.

Dillon's mother and he came up to me. She was playing peace-maker saying things like, "We don't know what's going on here, but we don't want any trouble…" I remember thinking, "Then your son shouldn't be riding in a way that brings trouble on."

Dillon tried to get in my face and lied about making me crash in that first turn. "I didn't make you crash, you just washed out, it had nothing to do with me." He then asked me why I took him out and what was up with me waiting on the top of the turn so I could do it again. He finally ended up walking away with an "attitude" after we both begrudgingly apologized to each other. I am thankful that our parents were there. If they weren't I would probably be feeling guilty for beating him up. The tension was that high.

I learn things in every race, but in that Golden State National I realized just how hard I could push the bike and myself. It turned me from a crazy, intense rider that was competitive into a rider with the skills of a true pro. And it paid off, big time.

The other races that I believe were extremely important in helping me become sponsored by Suzuki were the RM Cup Challenges at Glen Helen in San Bernardino, California. In these races all the riders are basically on the same equipment. There may be some minor differences in how the bikes are modified, but for the most part it is the best rider that wins. No one has any real advantage and it is only the riders' skills that can earn the victory. It was also my chance to show Team Suzuki that they should be sponsoring me, not Dillon Lord.

While I was training and getting ready for the Suzuki RM Cup that was coming up in a couple of weeks, our country was attacked. Everyone has their own personal memories of how September 11, 2001, affected them. Although I was still young, it hit me hard. It wasn't like I couldn't believe something like that could happen, it was I couldn't understand why. Those events on that historic day left a big mark on my inner core. I remember wanting to do something to help people heal, but what? Then I remembered a commercial from a long time ago that had the patriotic jingle, "Baseball, hotdogs, apple pie and Chevrolet." It reminded me that Motocross is a truly American sport. Today there are races all over the world, but it did begin here in the United States even though most of the bikes we race are from overseas. I went out and picked up as many stickers of the American flag I could find and put them next to every place my number was. On my helmet, bike, and jersey there were flags on every open square inch. It made me feel like I was doing something to help. The warmest memory I have is when I saw many other riders putting flags on their stuff after they saw me do it. Dirt bikers are always competitive and always looking for angles to edge out the competition and there are not too many compliments thrown around. Seeing the American flags on all the other riders made me feel good on a couple of levels. First it made me proud of the sport and the people in it. Second, it showed me that the other riders paid attention to what I did. It showed me that I really was making a name for myself.

I felt that I was in the best shape I had ever been, both mentally and physically, at the start of the RM Cup, but when the gates dropped in the 125 class I got caught up in the crowd and had a bad start. More times than not, the winner of the race can be determined within the first few seconds after the gate drops and, believe me, I was now in no position to win. There were a lot of very talented riders in that race and fourteen of them were already ahead of me before the end of the first lap.

There are always reasons why I want to win, but this race provided extra motivation. When riders registered for the race, they would provide their bikes' vehicle identification numbers to Suzuki. If you came in first place, you would get more than two thousand bucks to spend at any Suzuki dealership. I wanted to win that money! It wasn't just the financial reward that excited me, it was the fact that I would beat all of Suzuki's best riders to get it.

I wish I could tell you that I came up from fifteenth place to win the race, but I didn't. I did, however, manage to finish third which was quite an accomplishment in itself and got some attention from Team Suzuki. It also reminded me of how important the start of each race was. If I had started in the top ten, maybe I would have walked away with the two thousand dollar winner's prize...

I got a chance to redeem myself later in the day in the 250 class. Every rider was on Suzuki RM 250s which are crazy powerful bikes. My family had bought mine not too long before this race and I have to admit that I wasn't entirely sure I had the experience to win on it yet. Then I saw Lord was also in this race. It gave me all the motivation I needed to give it my all on the track. I still held a grudge.

I got a much better start in this race and was in the top three right from the beginning. In a few short laps I passed Lord and the only thing between me and winning was one rider who was riding with the same intensity as I was. This track had a huge 180-foot jump that went right into a big turn. I knew that if I was going to have any chance of winning, it would be on this part of the track. The leader was taking the jumps low and fast trying to hold on to the lead. I would have to hit high and hard to set myself up on the turn to be in a spot where I could pass the other rider. Once again that inner demon or desire kicked in and I found myself way high on the turn pulling back on my bars trying to squeeze every milli-second out of my bike. It must have looked pretty impressive; that moment was replayed over and over again in the following months on all the sports channels. They showed me flying through the air and off the screen as the cameras focused on the leader. Then at the last moment I pop back onto the screen and pass up the other rider to win the race. It is still pretty cool to watch myself on the little screen, but it was very cool to become the Suzuki RM 250 Cup holder. I had gone up against all the best riders from all over the country. Most of Team Suzuki's riders were on the track also, but it was me, not them, that won the cup. This made it pretty hard for Suzuki to ignore me now.

I still had some work to do, but it was becoming clear that I would be getting a call from Suzuki very soon and it took a huge load off my shoulders — and also off my family's. I look back now and I can easily see how important that day was for me. The first race proved that I had heart as I gave it my all to win no matter what position I was in. The second race showed that I had what it took and the talent to win a big race. My confidence was already high. What was important was that the powers behind the decision of who to sponsor were now seeing it too.

I also had some fun. Like the first race, Suzuki offered a big cash prize for winning the cup. Later that week I went to the local shop and got some more stuff for my bike. I also bought my parents a high-end scooter. They still loved to go camping and they took it with them every time they went. They have it to this day and every time I go to their house and see it in the garage I can't help but to smile. It represents so much. Not only did it mark the point when I became a real player in the sport of motocross, it also helped me to give back to my family. It could in no way repay them for all they have done for me, but it was a start and it felt good to know I was giving back to them what they had always given me, a chance to have some fun.

CHAPTER 10
HEART

A t my core I know I am a success in motocross because I feel it where it counts. In my heart.

There are so many images the word "heart" congers up in people's minds, but for me it is the single most important part of my drive to succeed. I internalize my efforts as deep into my heart as I possibly can and that makes me more than motivated, it's more like obsessive. Sure, there were times that I would get discouraged. I sometimes felt like I was dragging a ton of dumbbells chained to my ankles as I walked through the gym doors, my body wasn't up for it. But in my heart, there was nothing that was going to stop me from getting a workout in. I knew that the better shape I was in, the more competitive I would be on the track.

There are a ton of athletes who put their heart into their professional careers, but motocross is a little different than most. It's not the only solo sport out there, but like in all racing, whether it be in cars or motorcycles or anything that requires man and machine to be top notch to be competitive, when the gate drops it is you and you alone that determine the result. At the beginning of my journey I had never tried to use the fact that I had to operate on a shoestring budget, which meant bikes that were not as good as most of the other riders, as an excuse for not winning. In fact, looking back now it made me better. I could have won more races if I had the best equipment, but not having it showed me how deep into my heart I could go to get the most out of me as a racer. It also gave me the discipline to go out and do the things I had to do to be the best. Working out, studying the tract to find the line for the most speed or anything at all I needed to have an edge over the other riders was a direct result of the heart I put into the sport. Sometimes equipment fails and there is nothing that can be done about it, but I resolved very early on that I was not going to be the reason for a loss. I would not let me or my ability accept anything less, and it was because of this that I have no regrets.

It worked like that in all aspects of the beginnings of my career. If things didn't go the way I wanted them to, I tried not to let them bring me down. Instead, I would look for a way to over-come challenges that came my way and there were plenty. I also think that by putting my heart fully into my career strengthened my family's resolve.

As I look back I am still blown away about how powerful my mom and dad's dedication to me and my dreams were. Even my siblings were always behind my efforts without waver. As I hear them all talk about it today, I can understand that it was the way I was putting my heart into my dreams that provided their motivation as much as my own.

About a year or two after my extended family helped to foot the bill for my racing I had built up a good reputation. I was get-ting a lot of attention from all of the industry's magazines and was being interviewed more than any of the other riders after the big races. I was wining all the time and became known as a rider that was fun to watch on the track. I was willing to push myself so hard, again because of that heart deal, people thought that my riding style was nothing short of crazy. It looked like I was totally out of control, but I wasn't, I was in complete control and calculating every moment on how to take the checkered flag.

I was enjoying the attention; I even got a new tag, "The Sleeper." The thinking was that I would come out of nowhere and win. But, to be honest, it was also frustrating at the same time. The reporters who interviewed me were the real experts; they knew all of the other riders and what it took to be successful in the sport. So when they stuck a microphone in my face or be jotting notes on their notepads and ask me that pesky little question I told you about before, "With all of your talent and dedication, why are you not sponsored?" it would bring me down a bit.

I was getting sick of hearing that question because I didn't have an answer. What sucked was when I would read the articles about me in the magazines. It was one thing to have to deal with the question, but having it scream from the pages in black and white was almost more than I could bear. It felt like I was dumped out naked on a street corner. The whole world of motocross was reading about my frustration and the fact that I wasn't where I should be. Sponsored. I always try to stay grounded and maintain a level head and keep my ego in check. But I knew that there was no good reason why I wasn't sponsored and on one of the bigger teams. I was as good, if not better, than most of the riders that were sponsored by the big time companies. I was faster, more fun to watch, and I consistently won more races. But here I was still having my family pay my way. Before, when I had to ride on inferior bikes, I could justify not being picked up by a sponsor. I didn't let it stop my pursuit of my dream, but that little tug of doubt was there from time to time. But now I had the equipment that was as good as any on the track and I was winning all the time. It was confusing and frustrating at the same time. And yes, it was a little heart breaking, also. But I still gave everything I had for the sport, and in every race I focused on what the future could hold and not on the past or present that wasn't exactly the way I wanted it to be.

Even though I enjoyed very bit of my journey, I have to be honest, there were times I did feel a little sorry for myself. Even though I was the rider to beat on many occasions, I was also the rider who showed up at the track with his name ironed on the back of his jersey in individual letters that were sometimes a little crooked. The sponsored riders had their jerseys custom made and their names looked like a Hollywood billboard compared to mine. They also sported a ton of different patches from the companies that were involved with the sport that they were riding for. They stood out as the true rock stars and kings of the track. It was about more than just bragging rights, those differences on just the jerseys we wore alone represented to the world who the true recognized pros were and made the other riders look and feel like groupies trying to get tickets to the backstage show, but always turned down. I know it might not sound like a big deal, but it affected me. I was getting tired of feeling like the overgrown Cub Scout at his first day of training standing next to an Eagle Scout with a chest full of merit badges, the difference being that I had earned all the badges, I just couldn't wear them. I had gotten to a point in my personal race to get sponsored that winning the championships wasn't enough. Yes, I could say I was a champion, but if I didn't get picked up by a substantial sponsor, I was going to know I failed.

What made things worse was when I tried to talk the team manager of Suzuki. He would give us the brush off every time my dad or I approached him to see if he would check me out. Part of me understood, part of me wanted to become enraged. I knew he was approached all the time by riders who had the same dreams and I also understood it must have driven him crazy. Now I was coming to him with a truckload of championship trophies under my belt, many of which were won at the cost of his team's riders. I was beating them and it wasn't just a once in a while fluke, I was consistently placing higher than any of his riders. But, I was still treated like the overachieving star-struck kid who was a nuisance. To say that I was becoming frustrated would be the understatement of the century. But, in my heart, I couldn't quit trying.

Then in 2003 I got the phone call.

I pray everyone can have a moment in their lives that is pure joy and exhilaration. The type of moment that stands out above all others and will be remembered with a euphoric happiness until one's last breath. A defining moment. Mine was when I got a call from the manager of Team Suzuki. "We are going to take a look at you for the team and pencil you in," was all he said, but he might as well have been Santa Claus with a sleigh full of dreams come true, just for me. I was barely old enough to vote, but I felt like I had been pushing, clawing and fighting for a lifetime to get that call. After I got it, I felt like I was a couple of feet taller. The feelings of joy swelled in the entire house. My sisters were screaming and my parents were fist pumping. The sense of accomplishment was completely overwhelming and the emotional impact oozed out of all of our pores. It was a moment I will never, ever forget.

It was late in the season when I got the call from the team manager and it wasn't clear if they wanted to start me right away or wait until the next season. I was chomping at the bit to get started, but also wanted to play by their rules. I didn't want to act like a prima donna right out of the gate. I was also considering how the team manager had said "penciled in." Pencils can be erased, I wanted it to be in permanent ink! So I called him back the next day and asked when he wanted me to start. I was relieved to hear the contracts were already on their way and he was getting it set up to have new bikes and equipment sent. I had hit the big time, but at that moment it didn't fully grasp how big it really was.

Soon after the contacts were signed the real fun began. I still cannot adequately describe the feeling of excitement that overcame me as I stood in my garage watching four new dirt bikes being delivered. I couldn't wait to bust open the crates and when I did I saw that the bikes already had all of the team logos painted on them. For so many years I would look up to the guys riding those bikes showing them to be pros. Now I had four of my own. Two 125s and two 250s, and they were mine. Seeing my name and number on then was mind-boggling.

My team manager sent me a list of companies that he worked with to get the rest of the equipment that I needed. I laughed when I first looked it over. On the list were companies I had called many times over the years to beg for discounts. Now as a sponsored rider for Team Suzuki, they didn't put me on hold. They talked to me like I was their most important customer and wanted to satisfy my needs. I even remember one that I had contacted just a few weeks before. Back then they treated me like I was a prank caller, now I was the king. I couldn't help myself and had to ask, "Do you remember talking to me a few weeks ago about the same stuff?"

"I'm sorry I do not remember that." Yea, right…

As I look back and see how different it is to be a sponsored pro compared to wanting to be, well let's just say it was a quantum leap. It was like having dinner at McDonald's compared to dining at the most posh and expensive restaurant in one of Vegas' top-end casinos with a team of waiters hanging on your every word. Instead of having fancy entrées on the menu, my list was a menu full of all of the top companies in the sport and all I had to do was pick up the phone and place my order. Instead of getting stuck with a huge bill at the end of the meal, I would get a nice check from many of the companies just for the honor of having me race with their stuff or wear a patch with their logo.

There were a few of the bigger companies that weren't on the list, so I called my team manager and asked him if he could help me. One that sticks out in my mind was FOX. Anyone who has spent any time around motocross knows that FOX is a huge name in the sport, so when I called my manager to see if he could set me up with them and he said he would get back to me. I figured that maybe it wouldn't work out. I was still too new. Twenty minutes later he called me back and gave me the contact info. Later that day I was ordering goggles and other equipment from FOX and they soon became one of my biggest sponsors. I couldn't believe it and my excitement ran all the way down to my "lizard brain." EVERYONE in the sport wants to be sponsored by FOX.

It was literally overnight that I had gone from a wanna-be who was calling around begging for discounts so I could be competitive in the races, to a pro who was having everything I needed sent to me at no charge and many times with a check to show their appreciation. Coming up through the ranks I thought I had an idea what it would feel like to be a sponsored pro, but to be honest, I wasn't even close. If I had known what it was really like, I might have tried harder. I don't know how, I was giving it my all, all of the time.

The feelings of accomplishment were overwhelming. I remember feeling lightheaded as I made the decisions of what I needed, picked up the phone and placed the order to companies I had been pining after for so long. Just a week before I was struggling trying to figure out why I had not been sponsored yet and wondering how much longer I had to make it happen. In an instant I went from being fearful that the dream may never come true to being intimidated that it had.

I have heard it said many times that the thrill is in the chase, but I have to tell you, it wasn't like that for me. The thrill was seeing the contact in front of me that was the proof that my dreams had come true and goals accomplished. After a race I experience an adrenaline crash. At the drop of the gates, you go from zero to whatever it takes to win in an instant. At the end you have to come back down to earth and become a normal human being again. Part of you misses the excitement that was there a few moments before. This time I was looking forward to the future as I signed the contract. I had paid the price and I still had more to prove to both the fans and myself. There was no looking back.

Well, almost. As happy as I was to finally achieve the dream, I still had to wonder why it took so long. I explained to you earlier that getting sponsored by the factory teams was not just about winning and being the best rider out there. It is not that simple, but I wish it were. For every sponsored rider there are at least a hundred good riders chasing the dream and they don't get picked up for many reasons. There are politics, who you know and a ton of other variables that go into the equation. You have to remember that everything I have described to you in this book, except for my injuries, took place before I was on the planet for a full two decades. I was tempted to ask my new team manager why he didn't pick me up sooner, but thought better of it. I was the new guy and I didn't want to make any waves. I just wanted to race as a factory sponsored rider.

Maybe it was because I was too young. I was racing motocross before I was old enough to drive a car. I might have rubbed someone the wrong way. I had a few friends think out loud that the fact that I was doing so well out there made the factory teams nervous, no one likes seeing their guys get beat by a no-name. It could have been the sponsors thought that I was not ready for the responsibility that comes with being a sponsored pro. Whatever the reason for the delay, it didn't matter. I chose to focus on the fact that I had truly made it and looked forward to the challenges I would face in the races to come. Some people might say that I finally got lucky, but I would tell you that I was truly blessed.

I clearly remember sitting back in my chair and closing my eyes, reliving every aspect of my career up to that point. All of the crashes and disappointments. All of the victories and fun. All of the laughter and tears I shared with my family. I could feel the grips of the handlebars of the first dirt bike my dad brought home years before and my stomach remembered the butterflies when I took my first jump. It was less than a foot off the ground, but I got to tell you, at the time it felt the same as the hundred foot jumps I take today. I guess it is all relative. I remembered all of the races that I had won and lost, and all of the emotions that came with both. There was not a happier or more thankful guy on the planet, but I didn't get it until a few days later.

A package came in the mail and I had no idea what it was. As I opened it I could see that it was my new jersey for team Suzuki. My heart beat faster as I pulled it out of the box and checked the front of it out. I smiled as I saw all of the patches from the companies that were now sponsoring me were plastered all over it. I had never felt so blessed.

I got up out of my chair and started across the room to hang up my new jersey in the closet, smiling ear to ear. I couldn't help it. I knew from this point forward I was going to race as the sponsored professional motocross racer that I always wanted to be and it felt good. Really good. But, for some reason I remembered the day my dad carried me off the track and the tears running down his cheek. It was just one of the days we thought the dream was lost. It was by far the most emotional moment of my journey. I understoond all of the sacrifices it took to get here, by all of us. I had been so focused on the goal that I forgotten some of the setbacks. Then I grabbed the hanger and gently placed the jersey on it. As I hung it up I saw its back for the first time. Printed on the nylon in bold print was, "Team Suzuki" and right there above it in perfect Hollywood billboard style was "*COSTELLA.*" It was for completely different reasons and totally contrasting emotions, but this time it was my turn shed a tear. Okay, maybe a few.

Made in the USA
Las Vegas, NV
17 May 2024

90040307R00066